The
Unofficial Handbook
of the United Church of Christ

About the Peace Sign Pilgrim

The UCC is all about holding differences in tension: old/new, conservative/liberal, serious/funny. The Peace Sign Pilgrim embodies some of these tensions and seeks to honor the serious, holy lives of our founders and the progressive, God Is Still Speaking flavor of the United Church of Christ by combining them into one.

Even though theology is serious stuff, we should nonetheless remember that it is not our theology that saves us, but Jesus Christ. Therefore, our life in the church can be buoyant, and our theological wrangling can be done with a sense of humor and love for our neighbor.

The
Unofficial Handbook
of the United Church of Christ

Quinn G. Caldwell
and Curtis J. Preston

UNITED
CHURCH
PRESS ®
Cleveland

United Church Press
700 Prospect Avenue
Cleveland, Ohio 44115-1100
unitedchurchpress.com

Scripture quotations are from the New Revised Standard Version of
the Bible, copyright © 1989, Division of Christian Education of the
National Council of the Churches of Christ in the United States of
America.

Part of this book was originally published as the *Lutheran Handbook* ©
2005, Augsburg Fortress. Used with permission.

Pages 60–70: Sources for the charts include reference materials from
Information Please,® New York Times Public Library/Hyperion, Rose
Publishing, Time-Life, and Wadsworth Group/Thomas Learning.

Printed in the United States of America on acid-free paper

17   5

Library of Congress Cataloging-in-Publication Data
Caldwell, Quinn, 1977–
     The unofficial handbook of the United Church of Christ /
Quinn Caldwell and Curtis Preston.
        p.   cm.
     ISBN 978-0-8298-1875-8 (alk. paper)
     1. United Church of Christ.   I. Preston, Curtis, 1976–   II. Title.
BX9885.C35 2011
285.8′34 – dc22   2011013135

Contents

This Book Belongs to . . .

Name _____

Address _____

_____

Email Address _____

Telephone _____

Birth Date _____

Baptismal Birth _____

First Communion _____

Confirmation Date _____

Godparents' Names (baptismal sponsors)

_____

_____

_____

_____

Churches I've Belonged To: Years of
                                          Membership

_____   _____

_____   _____

_____   _____

_____   _____

_____   _____

About My Congregation

Name _____

Address _____

Year Organized/Founded _____

My Pastor(s) _____

_____

_____

_____

Number of Members _____

Average Weekly Worship Attendance _____

Facts about My Denomination _____

_____

_____

_____

_____

_____

Other Information about My Congregation and Faith

_____

_____

_____

_____

Preface

Please Be Advised:

Lots of books, pamphlets, and booklets have been written through the centuries as companions for average folks who wanted help navigating their way through a complicated subject. *The Boy Scout Handbook* comes to mind, for example. So do *The American Red Cross First Aid and Safety Handbook, Tune and Repair Your Own Piano: A Practical and Theoretical Guide to the Tuning of All Keyboard Stringed Instruments,* and *National Audubon Society's Field Guide to North American Reptiles and Amphibians.* They stand as testimony to the average person's need for a guide to both the vast truths and complex detail that make up a particular area of interest. These books turn complicated, inaccessible ideas into simple, easy-to-understand concepts, and, if necessary, into action steps that are easy to follow.

Likewise, *The Unofficial Handbook of the United Church of Christ* follows this format. Here you will find a combination of reliable, historical, and theological information alongside some fun facts and very practical tips on being a churchgoing follower of Jesus Christ, all presented in a down-to-earth, tongue-in-cheek sort of way.

You will also discover that this book is intended for both learning *and* enjoyment. (Some of us have trouble doing the latter until we've suffered through the former. We say, if laughter's not the best teacher, it's right up there.) It's meant to spur conversation, to inform and edify, and to make you laugh. Think of it as a comedian with a dry sense of humor and a degree in theology. It can be used in the classroom with students or at the dinner table with family or in solitude.

But however you use it, use it! The point is this: being a follower of Jesus is hard enough without having to navigate the faith journey — let alone the maze of church culture — all alone. Sooner or later everyone needs a companion, and a laugh.

The Editors

Church Stuff

Every well-prepared churchgoer should have a basic understanding of Christian teachings and where they came from.

Plus, since every church goes about worship in a slightly
different way, it might take a little time to get the hang
of things — especially if you're new to a congregation. This
section includes:

- ♦ Essential facts about the Christian faith.

- ♦ Practical advice for singing hymns, taking communion,
  and getting to know the people in your congregation.

- ♦ Hints for enjoying worship — even when you're having
  a bad day.

How to Get to Know Your Pastor

Pastors play an important role in the daily life of your congregation and the community. Despite their churchly profession, fancy robes, and knowledge of Greek, pastors experience the same kinds of ups and downs as everyone else. They value member efforts to meet, connect with, and support them.

❶ Connect with your pastor after worship.
After the worship service, join others in line to shake the pastor's hand. Sharing a comment about the sermon, readings, or hymns lets the pastor know that his or her worship planning time is appreciated. If your congregation doesn't practice the dismissal line, find other ways to make that personal connection.

❷ Pray daily for your pastor, because he or she doesn't work just on Sunday.
Your pastor has many responsibilities, like visiting members in the hospital, writing sermons, and figuring out who can help drain the flooded church basement. In your prayers, ask God to grant your pastor health, strength, and wisdom to face the many challenges of leading a congregation.

❸ Ask your pastor to share with you why he or she entered ordained ministry.
There are many reasons why a pastor may have enrolled in seminary to become an ordained minister. Be prepared for a story that may surprise you.

❹ Stop by your pastor's office to talk, or consider making an appointment to get to know him or her.

Pastors welcome the opportunity to connect with church members at times other than worship. As you would with any drop-in visit, be sensitive to the fact that your pastor may be quite busy. A scheduled appointment just to chat could provide a welcome break in your pastor's day.

Getting to know your pastor can help you to get more out of church

How to Survive for One Hour in an Un-Air-Conditioned Church

Getting trapped in an overheated sanctuary is a common churchgoing experience. The key is to minimize your heat gain and electrolyte loss.

❶ Plan ahead.
When possible, scout out the sanctuary ahead of time to locate optimal seating near fans or open windows. Consider where the sun will be during the worship service and avoid sitting under direct sunlight. Bring a bottle of water for each person in your group.

❷ Maintain your distance from others.
Human beings disperse heat and moisture as a means of cooling themselves. An average-size person puts off about as much heat as a seventy-five-watt light bulb. The front row will likely be empty and available.

❸ Remain still.
Fidgeting will only make your heat index rise.

Use your bulletin as a personal fan to keep cool.

❹ Think cool thoughts.
Your mental state can affect your physical disposition. If the heat distracts you from worship, imagine you're sitting on a big block of ice.

❺ Dress for survival.
Wear only cool, breathable fabrics.

❻ Avoid acolyte or choir robes when possible.
Formal robes are especially uncomfortable in the heat. If you must wear one, make sure to wear lightweight clothes underneath.

❼ Pray.
Jesus survived on prayer in the desert for forty days. Lifting and extending your arms in an open prayer position may help cool your body by dispersing excess heat. If you've been perspiring, though, avoid exposing others to your personal odor.

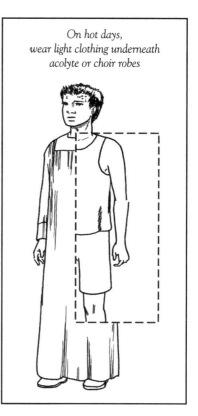

On hot days, wear light clothing underneath acolyte or choir robes

Be Aware

- Carry a personal fan — or use your bulletin as a substitute.

- Worship services scheduled for one hour sometimes will run long. Plan ahead.

How to Respond
When Someone Sits in Your Pew

We all carry a bubble of personal space. For some people, it's several feet. For others, it's about a millimeter. Wherever on the spectrum you happen to fall, there are certain situations in which we invite visitors into our little sphere of experience — like at church. Furthermore, human beings are territorial in nature and sometimes see strangers inside the bubble as an affront. These situations need not be cause for alarm.

1 **Smile and greet the "intruders."**
Oftentimes they are visitors to your congregation — new blood. Avoid creating bad blood you might regret later on. Make solid eye contact so they know you mean it, shake hands with them, and leave no impression that they've done something wrong.

2 **View the "intrusion" as an opportunity.**
Remember, you don't own the pew; you just borrow it once a week. Take the opportunity to get out of your rut and sit someplace new. This will physically emphasize a change in your perspective and may yield new spiritual discoveries.

3 **If you can tell that your new friends feel uncomfortable at having displaced you, despite your efforts to the contrary, make an extra effort to welcome them.**
Consider taking them to brunch after church to become acquainted. If there are too many for you to foot the bill, consider inviting them to accompany you on a "go Dutch" basis. This will eliminate any hierarchy and place you on equal footing.

How to Use a Worship Bulletin

Many UCC congregations offer a printed resource called a bulletin to assist worshipers. The bulletin may contain the order of the service, liturgical information, music listings, the day's Bible readings, and important community announcements.

❶ Arrive early.
A few extra minutes before worship will allow you to scan the bulletin and prepare for the service.

❷ Receive the bulletin from the usher.
Upon entering the worship space, an usher will give you a bulletin. Some congregations stack bulletins near the entrance for self-service.

❸ Review the order of worship.
When seated, open the bulletin and find the order of the service, usually printed on the first or second page. Some churches print the entire service in the bulletin so worshipers don't have to switch back and forth between worship aids.

❹ Determine if other worship resources are required.
The order of worship may specify additional hymnals, song sheets, candles, or other external supplies required during the service.

❺ Fill out the attendance card.
A card may be located inside the bulletin or somewhere in your row. Fill it out completely. You may be asked to pass this card to an usher or to place it in the offering plate. Some congregations have visitors/communion attendance books for people to sign.

6 **Reflect on bulletin artwork.**
Covers often feature a drawing or design that corresponds
to the season of the church year or the day's Bible verses.
Examine the artwork and make a note of its connection
to the lessons or sermon.

7 **Track your worship progress.**
The bulletin will guide you through the liturgy, hymns,
and lessons as you worship and let you know where you
are at all times.

8 **Watch for liturgical dialogues.**
The bulletin may contain spoken parts of the liturgy not
found in the hymnal. The worship leader's parts may be
marked with a "P:" or "L:". The congregation's responses
may be marked with a "C:" and are often printed in
boldface type. "One" and "Many" may also be used.

9 **Identify the worship leaders and assistants.**
The names of ushers, musicians, greeters, readers, acolytes,
and pastors usually can be found in the bulletin. Greet
these people by name following the service. Make good
eye contact.

10 **Review the printed announcements.**
Community activities, calendars, and updates are often
listed in the back of the bulletin. Scan listings during the
prelude music, the offering, or the spoken announcements.

11 **Make good use of the bulletin after the service.**
Some congregations re-use bulletins for later services.
Return the bulletin if possible. Recycling bins may also be
provided. If you wish, or unless otherwise instructed, you
may take the bulletin home with you.

Be Aware

- Bulletins often use letter or color codes to signify which hymnals should be used. Look for a key or legend that details this information.

- Many church secretaries and worship committees need help preparing the bulletin each week. You may want to volunteer to copy, fold, or assemble the bulletin for an upcoming service.

- Most congregations stand at certain times during worship, such as to honor Jesus' presence when the gospel is read. Standing and sitting — even occasional kneeling — aren't for exercise. Rather, they're an important physical participation in worship that helps you focus on the meaning behind the action.

If you choose not to save your worship bulletin, be sure to recycle it whenever possible.

How to Sing a Hymn

Music is an important part of the UCC tradition and an enjoyable way to build community. Many people find that singing and music touch them in ways that words alone do not. When singing together, the church becomes the Body of Christ — we even breathe at the same time!

❶ Locate hymns in advance.

As you prepare for worship, consult the worship bulletin or the hymn board on the wall to find numbers for the day's hymns. Bookmark these pages in the hymnal using an offering envelope or attendance card.

❷ Familiarize yourself with the hymns.

Examine the composer credits, the years the composers lived, and whether the tune has a different name than the hymn itself. Note how the hymn is categorized in the hymnal. Many hymnals group the songs into categories, such as "Opening Hymns," "Christmas," etc.

❸ Assist nearby visitors or children.

Using a hymnal can be confusing. If your neighbors seem disoriented, help them find the correct pages, or let them read from your book.

❹ Adopt a posture for best vocal performance.

Hold the hymnal away from your body at chest level. Place one hand under the spine of the binding, leaving the other hand free to turn the pages. Keep your chin up so your voice projects outward. Smile (unless the hymn is about the Crucifixion; in that case, hold off on the smiling till you get to the Resurrection part).

❺ Overcome your issues.
Feel yourself standing there with an open hymnal, staring around with a stony look on your face instead of joining in. Take a moment to wallow in whatever it is that usually keeps you from singing in church: the memory of the time somebody said you have a bad voice, your fear of not doing it right, your belief that singing isn't manly, your "nobody can make me do what I don't want to do" attitude. Enjoy those old familiar feelings. Then get over them. The church needs your voice.

Support the hymnal's spine with one hand. Place the other on the open page.

❻ Begin singing.
If the hymn is unfamiliar, sing the melody for the first verse, then explore the written harmony parts during the remaining verses. If you have no idea what we just said, just listen to the organ or piano and do your best to follow along boldly. Loud-singing neighbors may or may not be in tune, so follow them with caution.

❼ Focus on the hymn's content.
In a well-planned service, the lyrics will connect with a Scripture reading or other important theme of the day. Certain ones may be especially inspiring.

8 Avoid dreariness.

Hymns are often sung in such a serious way that the
congregation forgets to enjoy the music. Sing with energy.
If you find yourself in a church with an organist or pianist
that plays every hymn like a dirge, resist the urge to
yell, "Pick up the tempo!" Instead, consider making an
appointment with the musician to voice your concerns.

Be Aware

◆ Hymnals are not for use just at church; many also contain
prayers or readings for home use. Consider keeping a
personal copy of your congregation's hymnal at home for
further reference and study. Hymnals also make excellent
baptism or confirmation gifts.

◆ Some hymns use words and phrases that are difficult to
understand (such as "Here I raise my Ebenezer" from
the hymn "Come, Thou Fount of Every Blessing"). Use
a dictionary or a Bible concordance to clear up any
uncertainty. Or just make up your own meaning. It may be
less orthodox, but it's a lot more fun, and that's what most
people around you are probably doing, anyway.

A Note on UCC Hymnals

Each church in the UCC makes its own decisions about what hymnals to use. Herewith, a glance at a couple of the most common:

+ *The New Century Hymnal* (NCH), published in 1995. Bound in black; the avante garde choice. Groundbreaking and controversial for modernizing the language of old favorites, for using both masculine and feminine images for God, and for gender-neutral language for humans. If you know lots of hymns already, be prepared for some surprises as you sing. Before getting huffy about the changes, take a moment to try to understand why the editors might have made them — *then* huff away. Churches that use the NCH are often working hard to be forward-thinking and up to date.

+ *The Pilgrim Hymnal* (PH), published in 1958. Bound in red or blue; the traditional choice. Beloved by generations and full of all your old favorites in the language you grew up with — which, depending on your childhood experience of church, may or may not work for you. You can't necessarily tell much about a church by the fact that it uses the PH. It might be very traditional, or it might think that some of the changes in the NCH are clunky and inelegant. Or they might just be too poor to buy new hymnals.

Some churches use both the PH and the NCH, switching between them for different hymns. These churches inevitably have a mixture of strong traditionalist and avante garde people. This could be a sign of happy compromise and integration — or of split factions. Keep your eyes open!

Many churches use neither hymnal, having chosen one from another denomination or tradition. Remember, that's completely kosher in the UCC.

How to Sing a Praise Song

Some United Church of Christ congregations use modern worship styles, often called Praise & Worship (P&W), featuring guitars and drums. In these settings the words are typically displayed on large, multimedia projection screens.

❶ Follow the instructions of the song leader.
Someone in the praise band will invite the congregation to stand up, sit down, repeat certain sections, or divide into men's and women's vocal parts. Pay attention to this person to avoid getting off track.

❷ Learn the melody and song structure.
Pay special attention to the melody line sung by the band's lead vocalist. *Sing! Prayer and Praise,* the UCCs song book, is a great guide. Praise & Worship songs, however, can be tricky because they are rarely printed with notated sheet music and are sung differently from place to place.

❸ Sing along with gusto.
Once the melody has been introduced, join in the singing. When you're comfortable with the song, experiment with harmony parts.

❹ Avoid "zoning out."
Singing lyrics that are projected on giant screens can result in a glazed-over facial expression. Avoid this by surveying the worship area, noticing paraments and liturgical symbols, and making eye contact with other people.

❺ Identify lyrical themes.
Determine if the song is being used as a confession, a prayer, a hymn of praise, or serves another purpose.

❻ Watch out for raised hands.

Some UCCers emote while singing contemporary Christian songs and may suddenly raise their hands in praise to God. Be sure to give these worshipers plenty of room to avoid losing your eyeglasses.

Be Aware

◆ The praise band is there to help you and the congregation to sing and participate in worship, not to perform a concert.

◆ There are no strict prohibitions in the UCC tradition against physical expression during worship.

◆ In some congregations, praise gestures will draw amused stares.

Beware of especially passionate worshipers who might raise their hands too quickly.

How to Listen to a Sermon

Members of the UCC believe God's Word comes to us through the sacraments and the preaching of Holy Scripture. Honoring God's word, not to mention getting something out of church, includes diligent listening to the sermon and active mental participation.

❶ Review active listening skills.
While the listener in this case doesn't get to speak, the sermon is still a conversation. Make mental notes as you listen. Take notice of where and why you react and which emotions you experience.

❷ Take notes.
Note-taking promotes active listening and provides a good basis for later reflection. It also allows you to return to confusing or complicated parts at your own leisure. Some congregations provide space in the bulletin for notes, and many confirmation ministries provide structured worksheets.

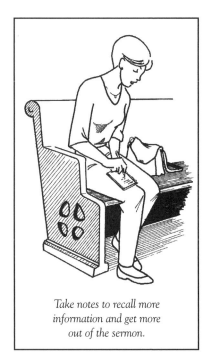

Take notes to recall more information and get more out of the sermon.

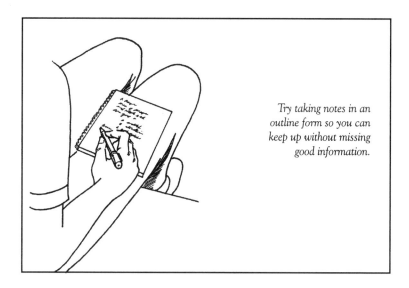

Try taking notes in an outline form so you can keep up without missing good information.

❸ Maintain good posture. Avoid slouching.

Sit upright with your feet planted firmly on the ground and your palms on your thighs. Beware of the impulse to slouch, cross your arms, or lean against your neighbor, as these can encourage drowsiness. Good pastors will be paying attention to people's faces to gauge the congregation's reactions. If her or his eyes fall on you, make steady eye contact.

❹ No sleeping!

If you find yourself falling asleep Sunday after Sunday, try getting more sleep the night before. If sitting and sleeping go hand in hand for you, you might be a great candidate to be an usher in your church. Sleeping while standing is considerably more difficult (and more dangerous) so if the problem continues, definitely give up ushering. If that doesn't work, the problem might not be yours; consider having the pastor fired.

❺ Listen for the law.
You may feel an emotional pinch when the preacher names the sinner in you. Pay attention to your reaction, and try to focus on waiting for the gospel rather than becoming defensive.

❻ Listen for the gospel.
Many sermons consist of "points" that follow each other as "one," "two," "three." Concentrate on the main heading of the point as you hear the pastor preach on each segment of the sermon. Other times, sermons follow more of a narrative or story approach. Either way, listen carefully for good news, or "gospel." And remember, the "Good News" doesn't always "feel" good. Sometimes it bites! Not every sermon contains good news, but every sermon that's from the Holy Spirit does.

❼ Review.
If you've taken written notes, read through them later that day or the next day. If you've taken mental notes, review them in a quiet moment. Consider sharing this review time with others in your congregation or household on a weekly basis.

❽ Be prepared to give immediate feedback to the preacher, as many churches will force you to walk by the minister as you exit the worship space.
Several options:

> If you liked the sermon, be prepared to say why. "Great sermon" is about as meaningful to hear as "Nice weather today." So if you liked it, you should know why and then say so.

> If you didn't like the sermon, several more options are open to you:

a. Comment on the prayers or other parts of the service

b. Say, "Interesting" or, "You gave us a lot to think about." While less direct, your preacher will surely get the point.

c. Try something like, "I'm sure you connected with someone this morning, it just wasn't me, but I'll still be back next week"

❾ Respond.

There are lots of ways to respond to a sermon. You might make a change in your behavior, your life, or the way you look at the world. You might recommit to old convictions. You might leave the church. Just remember: any time you really hear the gospel (which may not be every time you hear somebody preach!), it should call forth a response.

The Anatomy of a Baptism

Sponsors (godparents) may or may not be chosen and may or may not be on hand to support those being baptized and to make baptismal promises on behalf of children. The whole congregation joins in these promises and pledges their support also. Except in extreme circumstances, baptisms are not done in private; the whole church family needs to be there.

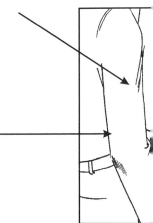

Water is the earthly element in baptism. You've heard God uses it to wash away sin, but that can be hard to swallow in the case of an infant who can't even sit up, much less sin. Try thinking of it like regular bathing or showering: you don't have to do it, lots of people choose not to do it, but for many it's an integral part of being healthy. Baptism is a one-time-only bath supercharged with God's Spirit. The baptizand will get dirty again, but by God's grace, the dirt won't stick.

Checklist for Baptism

❑ Person to be baptized
❑ Parent(s), if person to be baptized is a child
❑ Godparent(s), if desired
❑ Pastor
❑ Congregation
❑ Water
❑ The Holy Spirit

Pouring or sprinkling water on the baptized person, the pastor says something like, "I (or "we") baptize you in the name of the Father, and of the Son, and of the Holy Spirit." Some congregations will amend this language slightly to make it gender-inclusive.

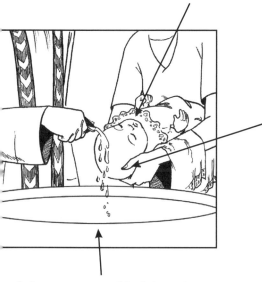

Pastors preside at baptisms to ensure good order. Thankfully you don't need a good pastor for a good baptism. Water + Holy Spirit = welcome to the family.

...er the baptism in water and God's Spirit, the pastor may trace ...cross on the baptized person's forehead, perhaps with oil, and ...lares that she or he now belongs to Christ.

Some congregations baptize adults and older children (but not babies!) by fully immersing them in an outdoor body of water or a large immersion tank inside a worship space.

Note: UCC congregations baptize people of all ages – not just infants. Adults and older children go through a process of prayer and study to prepare.

How to Respond to a Disruption during Worship

Disruptions during worship are inevitable. The goal is to soften their impact.

1 **Simply ignore the offending event, if possible.**
Many disruptions are brief and the persons involved act quickly to quiet them. Avoid embarrassing others; maintain your attention on the worship activity.

2 **Some disruptions cannot be ignored and may threaten to continue indefinitely. The agony will go on unless you act. Consider the following types:**

Active children

♦ *Your Problem:* You are most familiar with your own family. If you sense an outburst will end quickly, simply allow it to pass. If not, escort the child to the lobby for a little quiet time, then return.

Try to ignore worship interruptions you think will end soon.

- *Note:* Under all circumstances, children should be made to feel welcome in worship!

- *Someone Else's Problem:* Politely offer to help, perhaps by helping to occupy the child quietly or — with the parents' permission — by escorting the tot to the lobby, nursery, or cry room.

Personal electronics

- *Your Problem:* Turn off cell phones, pagers, and other electronic alarms immediately and discreetly. If contact is made and it is critical, remove yourself to the lobby and call back.

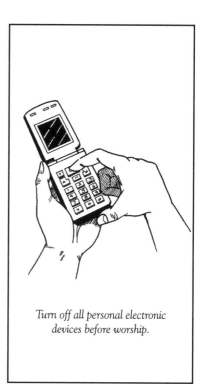

Turn off all personal electronic devices before worship.

Under no circumstances should you answer your phone during worship.

- *Someone Else's Problem:* Politely ask the person to respect worship by moving the conversation to the lobby.

Chatty neighbor

- *Your Problem:* Chatty persons should be alert to stares and grim looks from neighbors and be prepared to stop talking upon seeing them.

- *Someone Else's Problem:* Politely ask the talkers to wait until after worship to conclude the conversation. During the coffee hour, approach them with a cookie to mend any offense they may have felt.

Cameras

- *Your Problem:* Ask first if cameras are allowed. If so, unobtrusively and discreetly position yourself out of the line of sight of other worshipers. Flash cameras are strictly taboo.

- *Someone Else's Problem:* Politely offer to show the photographer where to stand to get the shot but without obstructing worship.

Sound system feedback

- Pastors often make jokes to cover for feedback and keep the appropriate mood for worship. If this happens, consider making a donation earmarked for a "new sound system" in the plate.

Be Aware

- Some people may perceive sneakers with light-up soles on acolytes and other worship assistants to be disruptive. If possible, coordinate the color of the shoe lights with the season of the church year to avoid undue flak.

How to Receive Communion

The Sacrament of Holy Communion (also called the Lord's Supper, the Eucharist, or simply the Meal) is a central event in UCC worship. All five senses are engaged in communion, and it is often the most interactive part of the service. Local customs for receiving communion can be confusing or complex, so it's wise to pay attention and prepare.

❶ Listen to the story.
One way or another, the story of the last supper Jesus had with his closest disciples, on which Communion is based, will be told. Listen to it carefully. Learn it by heart.

❷ Pray.
When the celebrant asks the Holy Spirit to enter the meal, add the strength of your prayer to the mix. Imagine the room filling up with love and power; ask God to make it so.

❸ Determine which method of distribution is used.
Verbal directions or printed instructions will likely be given prior to the distribution. Some congregations come forward to receive the elements (bread and wine or juice), symbolizing our movement toward God. Some congregations receive communion while seated in the pews ("sit and pass"). This way of receiving communion emphasizes (1) the importance of serving our neighbors as disciples of Christ and (2) that God (and not us) is the "actor" in the grace received through communion. All we have to do is receive it. Either way is theologically sound and historically precedented.

4 **Look for guidance from an usher.**
The usher will direct the people in each row or pew to stand and get in line.

5 **If invited to come forward, proceed to the communion station.**
If the congregation does "sit and pass" communion, wait for the elements to come to you, then receive them before passing them on.

6 **Eat. Drink.**

7 **Pray.**
While others are being served, hang out, listen to the music, pray for yourself or the world, and stay open to unexpected insights and images. You never know what God will do with an open heart!

Some Questions

What's for supper?

You've heard the bread called the Body of Christ before. Fear not; for most UCC congregations, this is symbolic language and the bread is just bread. The presence of the Body is all around and through the whole experience... including you! Any of the following might be used:

- Thin unleavened wafers, representing the unleavened bread that Jesus would have eaten at a Passover meal with his followers. Each person gets one.

- A common loaf, leavened or unleavened, representing the communal and familial aspects of the meal. Each person rips off a hunk for herself.

- Tiny squares of bread, representing...um...well, actually, nobody knows what this represents. Just take one and try not to think of it as a "crouton o' Christ."

- Some congregations offer a gluten-free alternative, such as a rice cracker, for those who need it.

Can you recommend a good wine to go with that?

Sure, but many UCC congregations use grape juice instead. Some use both and will tell you how to differentiate. We might call it the Blood of Christ, but the same applies here as with the bread. We serve it several ways:

- Small individual cups. This is the most common method in sit and pass. These are *not* shot glasses, so ignore your inner college student and try to partake with a little gravitas, okay? There will probably be a holder built into the pew in front of you for empties when you're done.

- A common cup, emphasizing the communal aspects of the meal. Each person takes a sip from the same large cup or chalice. If it's wine, see note about college students and gravitas above. If it's flu season, feel free to skip the cup and just eat the bread; either element alone is enough for God to fill you up with grace.

- Intinction, which is like the common cup minus the lip-touching and potential backwash. Each person dips their bread — not their fingers — into the cup, then eats. If you weren't paying attention and ate your bread too soon, or if you watched the dirty-fingernailed guy in front of you plunge his hand in up to the wrist, then see the note above about skipping the cup.

What can I say?

After receiving the elements, classic responses are "Amen" or "Thanks be to God." But if your innate politeness bubbles out as a "thank you," that's okay too; gratitude is appropriate.

Who can eat?

As a rule, UCC congregations welcome a wider range of feasters than many others, but different congregations have different policies on this. Some invite children to eat, some do not, some leave it up to parents to decide. Some require that one be baptized to join in; others think of the meal as a converting sacrament that might lead to baptism later. If you're unsure, ask your pastor. Pastoral blessings are often available for children or adults who are not communing.

What does it mean?

Again, different congregations differ, as do different worshipers. All congregations would agree that the Meal is one way God pours grace into the world, filling it up with love. Beyond that, ask your pastor if your congregation proclaims a specific meaning for Communion.

Once You Have Communed

♦ *Receive the post-communion blessing.* When everyone has been served, the presiding minister may bless the group or pray a prayer of thanksgiving.

♦ *Continue to participate when seated.* After returning to your place, you may join the congregation in singing the remaining communion hymns or pray in silence.

How to Pass the Plate

Passing the offering plate requires physical flexibility and an ability to adapt to differing practices. The offering is a practice that dates back to Old Testament times, linking money and personal finance directly to one's identity as a child of God. Giving of one's financial resources is an integral part of a healthy faith life.

1 **Pay close attention to instructions, if any.**
A service leader may announce the method of offering, or instructions may be printed in the worship bulletin or projected on an overhead screen.

2 **Stop digging in your wallet and pay attention to what's said about the offering.**
No pastor worth her or his salt will just stand up and say, "We will now receive an offering." They will likely also say some words designed to help you think about what you're doing. Resist the temptation to start going for the cash until after you've heard and digested this.

3 **Pray.**
Before deciding on an amount, ask God to show you how much to give today.

4 **Be alert for the plate's arrival at your row or pew.**
Keep an eye on the ushers, if there are any. In most congregations, guiding and safeguarding the offering plate is their job, so wherever they are, so is the plate. As the plate approaches you, set aside other activity and prepare for passing.

⑤ Avoid watching your neighbor or making judgments about her or his offering.

Many people contribute once a month by mail and some by automatic withdrawal from a bank account. If your neighbor passes the plate to you without placing an envelope, check, or cash in it, do not assume they didn't contribute.

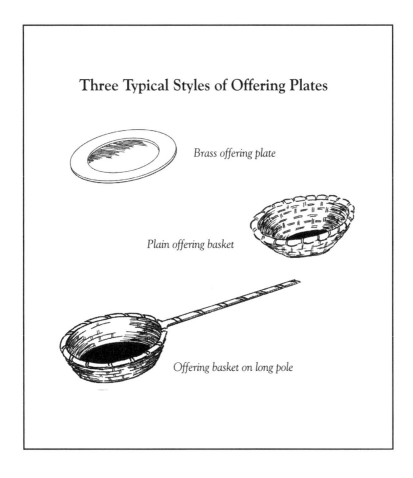

Three Typical Styles of Offering Plates

Brass offering plate

Plain offering basket

Offering basket on long pole

6 **Place your offering in the plate as you pass it politely to the next person.**
Do not attempt to make change from the plate if your offering is in cash. Avoid letting the plate rest in your lap as you finish writing a check. Simply pass it on and hand your check to an usher as you leave at the end of worship.

7 **Be sensitive to idiosyncrasies in plate types.**
Some congregations use traditional, wide-rimmed, felt-lined, brass-plated offering plates. Some use baskets of varying types. Some use cloth bags hung at the ends of long wooden poles that the ushers extend inward from the ends of the pews. Some congregations place the offering plate or basket at the rear of the worship space.

Be Aware

On pledging — It's a promise, not a bill

Each year your church will do a stewardship campaign. As part of this campaign, you will be asked to pledge a dollar amount for the coming year. Some things to think about:

• Stewardship is a church-word to describe the thoughtful use of God's abundant gifts. Caring for the earth and doling out dollars are both fundamentally about being smart with what God has given us.

• A pledge is a promise about how much you'll give to the church over the year. Many churches ask for pledges so they can make a best guess about the next year's budget. Imagine if your boss said, "I don't know how much we'll be able to pay you; I guess we'll just have to see what comes in." Thoughtful churches are making plans, and your pledge can help in the planning.

- Pledging helps you to be intentional with the money God's given you. If you commit a certain amount to the church, you're less likely to spend it impulsively on things that don't matter.

- You'll be more generous if you pledge than if you just dig in your wallet each week — we guarantee.

- You budget for everything else, don't you? Why not add a line item called "Building the Realm of God" right above "Cable bill" and "Vacation"?

- Think in terms of percentages of your total income. Ten percent, or a tithe, is the traditional amount to give, but if that doesn't work, start somewhere lower and aim to increase. And spare us the lengthy discussion of whether to use pre-tax or post-tax numbers to calculate it. Ask God to show you which is better.

- Give until it feels good. That's not to say your gift should be so small you don't notice it, but that it should be so big you feel like you're helping rebuild the world.

- Jesus said, "Where your treasure is, there will your heart be also." Where do you want your heart to end up?

How to Share the Peace in Church

In Romans 16:16 Paul tells members of the congregation to "greet one another with a holy kiss." The First Letter of Peter ends, "Greet one another with a kiss of love. Peace to all of you who are in Christ" (1 Peter 5:14).

Some UCCers worry about this part of the worship service due to its free-for-all nature. Some also feel uncomfortable because of their fear of being hugged. You can survive the peace, however, with these steps.

❶ Adopt a peaceful frame of mind.
Clear your mind of distracting and disrupting thoughts so you can participate joyfully and reverently.

❷ Determine the appropriate form of safe touch.
Handshaking is most common. Be prepared, however, for hugs, half-hugs, one-armed hugs, pats, and other forms of physical contact. Nods are appropriate for distances greater than two pews or rows. Or consider making a two-fingered peace sign.

❸ Refrain from extraneous chitchat.
Except in some very gregarious congregations, the sharing of the peace is not the time for lengthy introductions to new people, comments about the weather, or observations about yesterday's game. A brief encounter is appropriate, but save conversations for the coffee hour.

❹ Make appropriate eye contact.
Look the other person in the eye but do not stare. Looking the person in the eye highlights the relationship brothers and sisters in Christ have with one another.

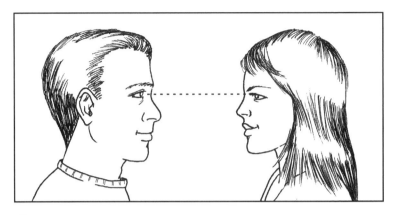

⑤ Declare the peace of God.
"The peace of the Lord be with you," "Peace be with you," "The peace of God," "God's peace," and "The peace of Christ" are ways of speaking the peace. Once spoken, the peace is there. Move on to the next person.

Be Aware

◆ Safe touch involves contact that occurs within your personal space but does not cause discomfort or unease.

How to Stay Alert in Church

❶ Get adequate sleep.
Late Saturday nights are Sunday morning's worst enemy.
Resolve to turn in earlier. A good night's sleep on Friday
night is equally important to waking rested on Sunday, as
sleep debt builds up over time.

❷ Drink plenty of water, though not too much.
It is easier to remain alert when you are well hydrated.
Consider keeping a small bottle of water with you during worship. One quick bathroom break is considered
permissible. Two or more are bad form.

❸ Eat a high-protein breakfast.
Foods high in carbohydrates force your body to metabolize
them into sugars, which can make you drowsy. If your diet
allows, eat foods high in protein instead, such as scrambled
eggs with bacon.

❹ Arrive early and find the coffee pot.

❺ Focus on your posture.
Sit up straight with your feet planted firmly on the floor.
Avoid slouching, as this encourages sleepiness. Good
posture will promote an alert bearing and assist in paying
attention, so you'll get more out of worship.

**❻ If you have difficulty focusing on the service, divert
your attention. Occupy your mind, not your hands.**
Look around the worship space for visual stimuli. Keep
your mind active in this way while continuing to listen.

7 **Stay alert by flexing muscle groups in a pattern.**
Clench toes and feet; flex calf muscles, thighs, glutei, abdomen, hands, arms, chest, and shoulders. Repeat. Avoid shaking, rocking, or other movements that attract undue attention.

8 **If all else fails, consider pinching yourself.**
Dig your nails into the fleshy part of your arm or leg, pinch yourself, bite down on your tongue with moderate pressure. Try not to cry out.

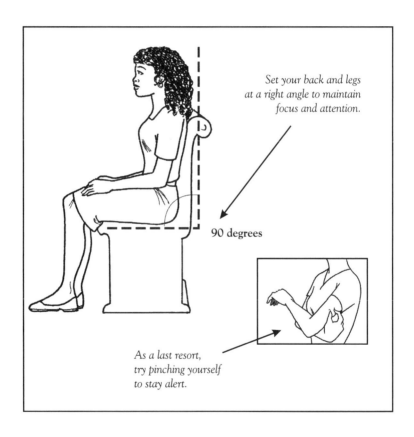

Set your back and legs at a right angle to maintain focus and attention.

90 degrees

As a last resort, try pinching yourself to stay alert.

What to Bring to a Church Potluck (by Region)

It is a generally followed practice in North American churches to enjoy three courses at potlucks (commonly referred to as "dishes"). Many of these dishes take on the flavor of the regions or cultures they represent. For best results, the preparer should understand the context in which the "dish" is presented.

The Salad

Potluck salads are quite different from actual salads. In preparation for making a potluck salad, ask yourself three questions:

+ Is this dish mostly meat-free?

+ Can this dish be served with a spoon or salad tongs?

+ Can it be served chilled?

If the answer is "yes" to any of these questions, consider the dish a potluck-eligible salad.

The mixture

This is the foundation of any potluck salad. It gives the salad a sense of direction. If at all possible, use ingredients that are indigenous to your area. For example, broccoli, lettuce, apples, macaroni, and candy bars are common in more temperate climates.

The crunchy stuff

This component gives life and pizzazz to an otherwise bland salad. Examples: tortilla chips, shoestring potato crisps, onion crisps, fried pigskins.

The glue

The glue holds the salad together. The variety of available types is stunning, ranging from a traditional oil-based salad dressing to mayonnaise and non-dairy whipped topping. Use your imagination. Consult regional recipes for exact ingredients.

Note: Some salads are best when made well in advance and allowed to sit overnight. This is called *marinating,* or "controlled decomposition." Do not use actual glue adhesive. Other salads are best prepared immediately before serving.

The Casserole

A three-layered dish, typically. In order to make each casserole as culturally relevant as possible, use the following guidelines. Consult local restaurants for ideas when in doubt.

Starch

East Coast: pasta or rice pilaf

Midwest: rice, potatoes, noodles, or more rice

South: grits

Southwest: black, red, or pinto beans

West Coast: tofu

Meat

East Coast: sausage or pheasant

Midwest: ground beef — in a pinch, SPAM luncheon meat

South: crawdad or marlin

Southwest: pulled pork

West Coast: tofu

Cereal

East Coast: corn flakes

Midwest: corn flakes

South: corn flakes

Southwest: corn flakes

West Coast: tofu flakes

Note: The starch and meat may be mixed with a cream-based soup. The cereal must always be placed on the top of the casserole.

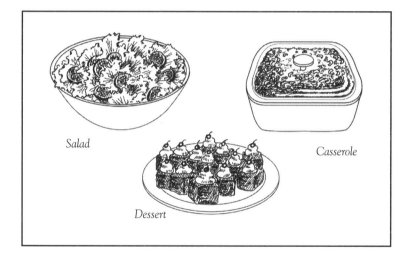

Salad

Dessert

Casserole

The Dessert

The most highly valued dish at a potluck, this can be the simplest and most fun to make. There are two key ingredients:

1. flour

2. fudge

Regional influences can be quite profound. The following are examples of typical desserts around the country. Consult your church's seniors for the nuances of your region.

Cleveland: fudge brownies with fudge frosting

Kansas City: triple-fudge fudge with fudge sauce and a side of fudge

Los Angeles: tofu fudge

Miami: fudge

New York City: cheesecake with fudge drizzle

Be Aware

◆ Use caution when preparing a dish. Adding local ingredients to any meat, salad, or dessert can increase the fellowship factor of your potluck exponentially. It also raises the risk of a "flop."

◆ Always follow safe food-handling guidelines.

◆ Any combination of flavored gelatin, shredded carrots, mini-marshmallows, and canned pears is an acceptable "utility" dish, should you be unable to prepare one from the above categories.

Four Things You Should Know about the Reformation

❶ Most people in medieval times had low expectations.
They didn't know anything about advanced medicine, modern psychology, or what it was like to live in a democracy. They didn't expect to live very long. They didn't think they had much power over their lives. And they didn't think being an "individual" was very important.

❷ The reformers were Catholic.
The reformers wanted to make changes within the one Christian church in Europe, but they wanted to stay Catholic. None of them ever expected that their actions would lead to the dozens of Christian denominations around today.

❸ People in medieval times weren't allowed to choose their own religion.
You could believe whatever you wanted, but you could practice only the faith your prince or king chose. After the Reformation, only the regions whose princes had signed the Augsburg Confession could practice any faith other than Catholicism.

❹ Reformers addressed a variety of issues.
Some reformers fought for these changes: separation of church and state, a mystical relationship with God, better educated priests, and more moral leaders in the church.

Five Facts about Life
in Medieval Times

❶ The Middle Ages lasted more than a thousand years.
By some counts, the medieval period (or Middle Ages)
covered an era that began around the year 391 (when
Christianity became the Roman Empire's only legal
religion) and ended around 1517.

❷ Life was nasty, brutish, and short.
People who survived childhood usually did not live long
past age forty. If disease or starvation didn't get you,
violence and warfare did. It's been estimated that during
the 1400s about one-third of Europe's population died of
bubonic plague. Sanitation was practically nonexistent.

*Road travel was
harsh and sanitation
was minimal during
the Middle Ages.*

❸ The Christian church grew larger, more influential, and more dominant.

Headquartered in Rome, the Western church became a superpower. Church and state became inseparable. At its height (ca. 1000–1300), "Christian Crusaders" battled with Muslims and others for control of the "Holy Land," Thomas Aquinas wrote his *Summa Theologica,* and hundreds of "heretics" were burned to death.

❹ The "Cult of the Saints" developed.

Over the centuries, a system grew in which the leftover good works (merits) of the saints could be distributed to others, with the pope in charge of this store (treasury) of good works.

❺ Humanist and Renaissance-age thinkers also worked for reform.

At the end of the Middle Ages, early reformers such as Jan Hus and Girolamo Savonarola confronted the church corruptions they saw. Hus was burned, and Savonarola was hanged. For other examples, see "History's Six Most Notorious Heretics" on page 58.

History's Six
Most Notorious Heretics

Though vilified by those who write history, heretics played a critical role in the church. They refined its message and forced the church to be honest with itself. But heretics usually payed the ultimate price, and often they were wrong.

❶ Hypatia of Alexandria (370–415)

Hypatia was an African philosopher, mathematician, physicist, astronomer, and director of Alexandria's library, once the largest in the world. Bishop Cyril of Alexandria, out of jealousy, declared her a heretic and ordered her to be tortured and burned at the stake, together with her writings. Her mistakes were to prefer study to marriage, to know more than the bishop, and to be a female teacher of males.

❷ Pelagius (354–418)

Pelagius was a Celtic monk who believed in the goodness of human nature and the freedom of human will. These beliefs led him to denounce the doctrine of original sin — a core tenet of the church — and suggest that human beings were equal participants in their salvation with Jesus Christ. The *Pelagianism* movement, named after him, was a strict teaching of self-reliance. When Pelagius taught that one could achieve grace without the church, he was excommunicated.

❸ Joan of Arc (1412–1431)

Joan was a French peasant girl who was able to hear heavenly voices that urged her to liberate her nation from the British occupation. She was nineteen when sentenced as a heretic and burned at the stake. Joan's fault was to be a better army leader than men. She is now a national hero.

❹ Girolamo Savonarola (1452–1498)

Savonarola's parents wanted him to be a physician, but this Italian youngster decided to be a Dominican monk and serve people who were poor. He preached against Pope Alexander VI and the powerful Medici family. Members of the wealthy church and society hung and burned him and then threw his ashes in the Arnos River to prevent him from having a restful place.

❺ Martin Luther (1483–1546)

Luther's father, a peasant and coal miner, wanted him to be a lawyer. Martin disappointed him and became an Augustinian monk. Emperor Charles V and Pope Leo X threw him out of the church and put a price on his head, but Luther continued serving the poor, preaching and living the Bible, and sharing hospitality at the family dinner table.

❻ Hatuey (?–1511)

This Native American leader from the Guahaba region escaped from Haiti to Cuba. The brave Hatuey was captured and declared a heretic. A priest wanted to baptize him in order for the Indian to get to heaven after being burnt. The Taino chief rejected the Christian rite when he heard that in heaven there would also be people from Spain.

Comparative Religions

	Baha'i	Buddhism	Christianity
Founder and date founded	Bahá'u'lláh (1817-1892) founded Babism in 1844 from which Baha'i grew.	Founded by Siddhartha Gautama (the Buddha) in Nepal in the 6th-5th centuries B.C.	Founded by followers of Jesus of Nazareth, a Palestinian Jew, in the early 1st century A.D.
Number of adherents in 2000	About 7 million worldwide; 750,000 U.S.	360 million worldwide; 2 million U.S.	About 2 billion worldwide; 160 million U.S.
Main tenets	The oneness of God, the oneness of humanity, and the common foundation of all religion. Also, equality of men and women, universal education, world peace, and a world federal government.	Meditation and the practice of virtuous and moral behavior can lead to Nirvana, the state of enlightenment. Before that, one is subjected to repeated lifetimes, based on behavior.	Jesus is the Son of God and God in human form. In his death and resurrection, he redeems humanity from sin and gives believers eternal life. His teachings frame the godly life for his followers.
Sacred or primary writing	Bahá'u'lláh's teachings, along with those of the Bab, are collected and published.	The Buddha's teachings and wisdom are collected and published.	The Bible is a collection of Jewish and Near Eastern writings spanning some 1,400 years.

Confucianism	Hinduism	Islam	Judaism
Founded by the Chinese philosopher Confucius in the 6th-5th centuries B.C. One of several traditional Chinese religions.	Developed in the 2nd century B.C. from indigenous religions in India, and later combined with other religions, such as Vaishnavism.	Founded by the prophet Muhammad ca. A.D. 610. The word *Islam* is Arabic for "submission to God."	Founded by Abraham, Isaac, and Jacob ca. 2000 B.C.
6 million worldwide (does not include other traditional Chinese beliefs); U.S. uncertain.	900 million worldwide; 950,000 U.S.	1.3 billion worldwide; 5.6 million U.S.	14 million worldwide; 5.5 million U.S.
Confucius's followers wrote down his sayings or *Analects*. They stress relationships between individuals, families, and society based on proper behavior and sympathy.	Hinduism is based on a broad system of sects. The goal is release from repeated reincarnation through yoga, adherence to the Vedic scriptures, and devotion to a personal guru.	Followers worship Allah through the Five Pillars. Muslims who die believing in God, and that Muhammad is God's messenger, will enter Paradise.	Judaism holds the belief in a monotheistic God, whose Word is revealed in the Hebrew Bible, especially the Torah. Jews await the coming of a messiah to restore creation.
Confucius's *Analects* are collected and still published.	The Hindu scriptures and Vedic texts.	The Koran is a collection of Muhammad's writings.	The Hebrew scriptures compose the Christian Old Testament.

World Religions

Listed by approximate number of adherents

Christianity	2 billion
Islam	1.3 billion
Hinduism	900 million
Agnostic/Atheist/Non-Religious	850 million
Buddhism	360 million
Confucianism and Chinese traditional	225 million
Primal-indigenous	150 million
Shinto	108 million
African traditional	95 million
Sikhism	23 million
Juche	19 million
Judaism	14 million
Spiritism	14 million
Baha'i	7 million
Jainism	4 million
Cao Dai	3 million
Tenrikyo	2.4 million
Neo-Paganism	1 million
Unitarian-Universalism	800,000
Rastafarianism	700,000
Scientology	600,000
Zoroastrianism	150,000

Family Tree of Christianity

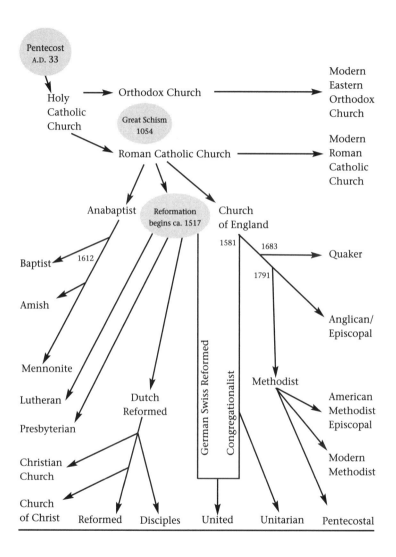

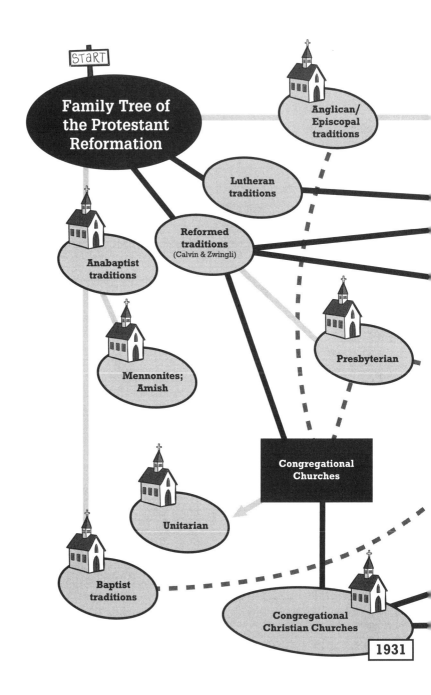

START

Family Tree of the Protestant Reformation

Anglican/ Episcopal traditions

Lutheran traditions

Reformed traditions
(Calvin & Zwingli)

Anabaptist traditions

Mennonites; Amish

Presbyterian

Congregational Churches

Unitarian

Baptist traditions

Congregational Christian Churches

1931

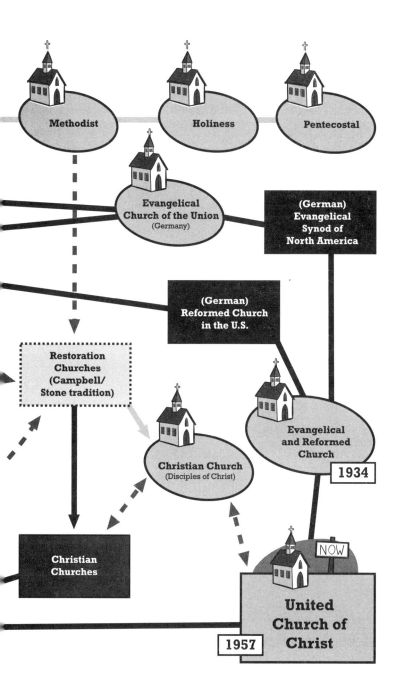

Methodist

Holiness

Pentecostal

Evangelical
Church of the Union
(Germany)

(German)
Evangelical
Synod of
North America

(German)
Reformed Church
in the U.S.

Restoration
Churches
(Campbell/
Stone tradition)

Christian Church
(Disciples of Christ)

Evangelical
and Reformed
Church

1934

Christian
Churches

NOW

United
Church of
Christ

1957

Comparative Denominations:

	Anglican	Catholic	Orthodox
Founded when and by whom?	1534: Henry VIII is declared head of the Church of England. 1549: Thomas Cranmer produces the first *Book of Common Prayer*.	Catholics consider Jesus' disciple Peter (died ca. A.D. 66) the first pope. Through Gregory the Great (540-604), papacy is firmly established.	A.D 330: Emperor Constantine renames Byzantium "Constantinople" and declares Christianity the empire's religion.
Adherents in 2000?	45-75 million worldwide; about 3 million U.S.	About 1 billion worldwide; 60 million U.S.	About 225 million worldwide; about 4 million U.S.
How is Scripture viewed?	Protestant canon accepted. Scripture is interpreted in light of tradition and reason.	The canon is 46 books in the OT (Apocrypha included) and 27 in the NT. Interpretation is subject to church tradition.	49 OT books (Catholic plus three more) and 27 NT. Scripture is subject to tradition.
How are we saved?	We share in Christ's victory, who died for our sins, freeing us through baptism to become living members of the church.	God infuses the gift of faith in the baptized, which is maintained by good works and receiving Penance and the Eucharist.	God became human so humans could be deified, that is, have the energy of God's life in them.
What is the church?	The body of Christ is based on "apostolic succession" of bishops, going back to the apostles. In the U.S., it is the Episcopal Church.	The mystical body of Christ, who established it with the pope as its head; he pronounces doctrine infallibly.	The body of Christ in unbroken historical connection with the apostles; the Roman pope is one of many patriarchs who govern.
What about the sacraments?	Baptism brings infant and convert initiates into the church; in Communion, Christ's body & blood are truly present.	Catholics hold seven sacraments. Baptism removes original sin; usually infants. The Eucharist undergoes transubstantiation.	Baptism initiates God's life in the baptized; adults and children. In the Eucharist, bread & wine are changed into body & blood.

Liturgical Churches

	Lutheran	Presbyterian	Methodist
Founded when and by whom?	1517: Martin Luther challenges Catholic teachings with his Ninety-five Theses. 1530: the Augsburg Confession is published.	1536: John Calvin writes *Institutes of the Christian Religion*. 1789: Presbyterian Church U.S.A. is organized.	1738: Anglican ministers John and Charles Wesley convert. 1784: U.S. Methodists form a separate church body.
Adherents in 2000?	About 60 million worldwide; about 9 million U.S.	40-48 million worldwide; 4 million U.S.	20-40 million worldwide; about 13 million U.S.
How is Scripture viewed?	Protestant canon contains 39 OT books, 27 NT. Scripture alone is the authoritative witness to the gospel.	Protestant canon accepted. Scripture is "witness without parallel" to Christ, but in human words reflecting beliefs of the time.	Protestant canon accepted. Scripture is primary source for Christian doctrine.
How are we saved?	We are saved by grace when God grants righteousness through faith alone. Good works inevitably result, but they are not the basis of salvation.	We are saved by grace alone. Good works result, but are not the basis of salvation.	We are saved by grace alone. Good works must result, but do not obtain salvation.
What is the church?	The congregation of believers, mixed with the lost, in which the gospel is preached and the sacraments are administered.	The body of Christ includes all of God's chosen and is represented by the visible church. Governed by regional "presbyteries" of elders.	The body of Christ, represented by church institutions. Bishops oversee regions and appoint pastors, who are itinerant.
What about the sacraments?	Baptism is necessary for salvation. The Lord's Supper is bread & wine that, with God's Word are truly Jesus' body & blood.	Baptism is not necessary for salvation. The Lord's Supper is Christ's body & blood, which are spiritually present to believers.	Baptism is a sign of regeneration; in the Lord's Supper, Jesus is really present.

Comparative Denominations:

	Anabaptist	Congregational	Baptist
Founded when and by whom?	1523: Protestants in Zurich, Switzerland, begin believers' baptism. 1537: Menno Simons begins Mennonite movement.	1607: Members of England's illegal "house church" exiled. 1620: Congregationalists arrive in the New World on the *Mayflower*.	1612: John Smythe and other Puritans form the first Baptist church. 1639: The first Baptist church in America is established.
Adherents in 2000?	About 2 million worldwide; about 600,000 U.S.	More than 2 million worldwide; about 2 million U.S.	100 million worldwide; about 30 million U.S.
How is Scripture viewed?	Protestant canon accepted. Scripture is inspired but not infallible. Jesus is living Word; Scripture is written Word.	Protestant canon accepted. Bible is the authoritative witness to the Word of God.	Protestant canon accepted. Scripture is inspired and without error; the sole rule of faith.
How are we saved?	Salvation is a personal experience. Through faith in Jesus, we become at peace with God, moving us to follow Jesus' example by being peacemakers.	God promises forgiveness and grace to save "from sin and aimlessness" all who trust him, who accept his call to serve the whole human family.	Salvation is offered freely to all who accept Jesus as Saviour. There is no salvation apart from personal faith in Christ.
What is the church?	The body of Christ, the assembly and society of believers. No one system of government is recognized.	The people of God living as Jesus' disciples. Each local church is self-governing and chooses its own ministers.	The body of Christ; the redeemed throughout history. The term *church* usually refers to local congregations, which are autonomous.
What about the sacraments?	Baptism is for believers only. The Lord's Supper is a memorial of his death.	Congregations may practice infant baptism or believers' baptism or both. Sacraments are symbols.	Baptism is immersion of believers, only as a symbol. The Lord's Supper is symbolic.

Non-Liturgical Churches

	Churches of Christ	Adventist	Pentecostal
Founded when and by whom?	1801: Barton Stone holds Cane Ridge Revival in Kentucky. 1832: Stone's Christians unite with Disciples of Christ.	1844: William Miller's prediction of Christ's return that year failed. 1863: Seventh-Day Adventist Church is organized.	1901: Kansas college students speak in tongues. 1906: Azusa Street revival in L.A. launches movement. 1914: Assemblies of God organized.
Adherents in 2000?	5-6 million worldwide; about 3 million U.S.	About 11 million worldwide; about 100,000 U.S.	About 500 million worldwide; about 5 million U.S.
How is Scripture viewed?	Protestant canon accepted. Scripture is the Word of God. Disciples of Christ view it as a witness to Christ, but fallible.	Protestant canon accepted. Scripture is inspired and without error; Ellen G. White, an early leader, was a prophet.	Protestant canon accepted. Scripture is inspired and without error. Some leaders are considered prophets.
How are we saved?	We must hear the gospel, repent, confess Christ, and be baptized. Disciples of Christ: God saves people by grace.	We repent by believing in Christ as Example (in his life) and Substitute (by his death). Those who are found right with God will be saved.	We are saved by God's grace through Jesus, resulting in our being born again in the Spirit, as evidenced by a life of holiness.
What is the church?	The assembly of those who have responded rightly to the gospel; it must be called only by the name of Christ.	Includes all who believe in Christ. The last days are a time of apostasy, when a remnant keeps God's commandments faithfully.	The body of Christ, in which the Holy Spirit dwells; the agency for bringing the gospel of salvation to the whole world.
What about the sacraments?	Baptism is the immersion of believers only, as the initial act of obedience to the gospel. The Lord's Supper is a symbolic memorial.	Baptism is the immersion of believers only. Baptism and the Lord's Supper are symbolic only.	Baptism is immersion of believers only. A further "baptism in the Holy Spirit" is offered. Lord's Supper is symbolic.

U.S. Christian Denominations

Listed by approximate number of adherents

Catholic	60 million
Baptist	30 million
Methodist/Wesleyan	13 million
Lutheran	9 million
Pentecostal/Charismatic	5 million
Orthodox	4 million
Presbyterian	4 million
Episcopalian/Anglican	3 million
Churches of Christ	3 million
Congregational/United Church of Christ	2 million
Assemblies of God	1 million
Anabaptist	600,000
Adventist	100,000

The Seasons of the Church Year and What They Mean

Advent is a season of longing and anticipation, during which we prepare for the coming of Jesus. The church year begins with Advent, as life begins with birth, starting four Sundays before Christmas. The liturgical color for Advent is blue, which symbolizes waiting and hope.

Christmas is a day and a season when we celebrate God's coming among us as a human child: Jesus, Emmanuel (which means "God with us"). The liturgical color for Christmas is white, which reminds us that Jesus is the Light of the world. Christmas lasts for twelve days, from December 25 to January 5.

Epiphany is celebrated on January 6, when we remember the three Wise Men's visit to the Christ child. The color for Epiphany Day is white. During the time after Epiphany we hear stories about Jesus' baptism and early ministry. The color for these Sundays is sometimes white and sometimes green. On the last Sunday we celebrate the Transfiguration. The color for this day is white, and we hear the story of Jesus shining brightly on the mountaintop.

Lent is a season when we turn toward God and think about how our lives need to change. This is also a time to remember our baptism, and how that gift gives us a new start every day! The color for Lent is purple, symbolizing repentance. Lent begins on Ash Wednesday and lasts for forty days (not including Sundays) and ends on the Saturday before Easter Sunday.

The Three Days are the most important part of the Christian calendar because they mark Jesus' last days, death, and res-urrection. These days (approximately three twenty-four-hour

The Seasons of the Church Year

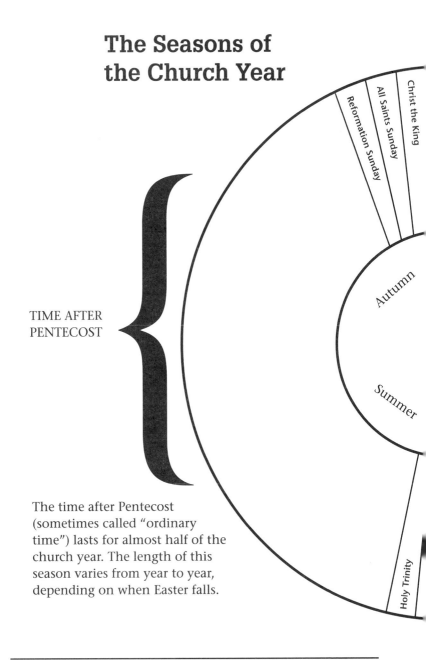

TIME AFTER
PENTECOST

The time after Pentecost (sometimes called "ordinary time") lasts for almost half of the church year. The length of this season varies from year to year, depending on when Easter falls.

Reformation Sunday

All Saints Sunday

Christ the King

Autumn

Summer

Holy Trinity

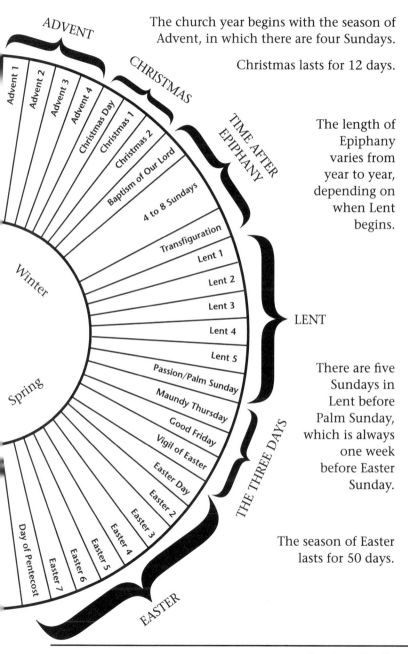

The church year begins with the season of Advent, in which there are four Sundays.

Christmas lasts for 12 days.

The length of Epiphany varies from year to year, depending on when Lent begins.

There are five Sundays in Lent before Palm Sunday, which is always one week before Easter Sunday.

The season of Easter lasts for 50 days.

periods) begin on Maundy Thursday evening and conclude on Easter evening. On Maundy Thursday we hear the story of Jesus' last meal with his disciples and his act of service and love in washing their feet. On Good Friday we hear of Jesus' trial, crucifixion, death, and burial. On Saturday, at the nighttime Easter Vigil, we hear stories about the amazing things God has done for us. It is a night of light, Scripture readings, baptismal remembrance, and communion — the greatest night of the year for Christians. On Easter Sunday we celebrate Jesus' resurrection and our new lives in Christ. Easter falls on a different date each year — sometime between March 22 and April 25.

Easter is not just one day, but a whole season when we celebrate the resurrected Jesus. The season begins on Easter Sunday and lasts for fifty days (including Sundays). The color is white, symbolizing resurrection and joy. The Day of Pentecost falls on the fiftieth day of the season (Pentecost means fiftieth), when we honor the Holy Spirit and the church's mission in the world. This day uses the fiery color of red.

Time after Pentecost is the longest season in the church calendar, lasting almost half the year. Sometimes this is called "ordinary time" because there aren't many special celebrations during these weeks. The liturgical color for the time after Pentecost is green, representing life and growth. Each week we hear a different story about Jesus' ministry from one of the four Gospels.

Special festivals are celebrated throughout the year. Some festivals occur the same time every year, such as Reformation Sunday (last Sunday in October) and All Saints' Sunday (first Sunday in November). Others, like saints' days, we might celebrate only when their day falls on a Sunday. The color for these days is either white or red.

In all cases, local traditions vary.

Everyday Stuff

Believing in God involves more than going to church and reading the Bible. It's about keeping your faith with you in every part of your life. This section includes:

- Advice for helping people in times of trouble.

- Tips on forgiving others and treating them with respect — even if you don't always feel like it.

- Suggestions for avoiding temptation on a daily basis. Some of these ideas go back to the Middle Ages.

How to Share Your Faith with Someone

Sharing the gospel with others is a natural part of exercising a mature faith. In fact, Jesus commanded his followers to do this, making it an important part of the life of faith (Matthew 28:18–20). Still, UCCers tend to be rather shy evangelists.

While "evangelism" has become a negative word for some people, sharing the story of salvation in Jesus Christ is still the most rewarding way to live out one's faith. It is also a discipline that takes practice.

❶ Look for the opening.
Regular daily conversations offer lots of chances to talk about your faith. Listen for open-ended comments, such as, "I wonder why life is like that," or, "Sometimes life seems so hard." When possible, offer a response from a Christian perspective. Begin sentences with phrases such as, "I've come to think..." or, "I don't have the perfect answer, but I believe..."

❷ Be yourself.
Expressing your faith should be natural and the same as other types of daily conversation. Avoid suddenly switching your tone of voice or vocabulary. Also, don't try to impress the other person with your knowledge. Allow the Holy Spirit to guide you.

❸ Watch for a chance to take the conversation deeper.
Carefully gauge the other person's response. Observe his or her facial expression, verbal tone, and body language. If he or she seems to be closing down, set the topic aside and wait for another time. If he or she keys in and perks up, be prepared to continue.

❹ Open up.
Human beings are attracted to each other by our strengths, but we bond because of our weaknesses. Key to sharing your faith is the willingness to be honest about your own life's struggles. This will communicate safety, which for many people is critical.

❺ Follow up.
Offer to continue the conversation later and arrange a time. At this point, the conversation will have become personally valuable to you. Allowing the person to see your commitment to your faith alongside your continuing questions will reassure him or her of your sincerity.

❻ Offer to share your faith community with the other person.
Most people join a church after being invited by a friend. When the time is right, invite the person to attend with you. Tell the person what makes it special to you.

❼ Try to maintain the relationship regardless of what the person does.
Be prepared for the other person to shut down around faith talk, decline your invitation to attend church, or even appear to avoid you. The most effective way to communicate that you're a follower of Jesus Christ is through your actions; continue to live naturally and with integrity. Watch for another opportunity to open the subject later on.

How to Pray

Prayer is intimate communication with God and can be used before a meal, at bedtime, during a worship service, or any time the need or opportunity arises. Silent and spoken prayers are both okay and may be used liberally throughout the day. Prayer is also taking time to listen to what God is saying to us. Spontaneous prayer is often best, but the following process may help build the habit.

1 Assess your need for prayer.
Take stock of the situation at hand, including your motivations. What are you praying for and why?

2 Select a type of prayer.
Prayers of supplication (requests for God's help), contrition (in which sin is confessed and forgiveness requested), intercession (on behalf of others), and others are good and time tested. Books of personal prayers, hymnals, and devotionals often contain helpful, prewritten prayers. Consider also an ad-libbed prayer from the heart.

3 Select a physical prayer posture.
Many postures are appropriate:

* The most common type of prayer in the New Testament is from a prone position, lying face-down on the ground, arms spread.

* Kneeling with your face and palms upturned is good for prayers of supplication.

* Bowed head with closed eyes and hands folded is common today and aids concentration.

There is no "official" posture for prayer. Choose your posture according to your individual prayer needs.

Choose a comfortable and appropriate posture for your prayer time

❹ Offer your prayer.
Pray with confidence. God listens to all prayer and responds. Breathe deeply, relax, and be open as the Spirit leads you.

❺ Listen.
Take time during your prayer simply to listen. Some prayer traditions involve only silent meditation as a means of listening for God's voice.

Be Aware

- ◆ God hears every prayer.

- ◆ Prayer can be done either alone or in the company of others (corporately).

- ◆ Environment matters. If possible, consider lighting a candle and dimming the lights to set the correct mood and help block out distractions.

How to Work for Peace and Justice on Behalf of People Who Are Poor and Oppressed

Knowing that good works are the result — not the cause — of salvation, UCCers have a long and extraordinary record of working for economic justice and relief around the world.

UCC congregations around the country have also set justice as one of their highest priorities, giving time and money both locally and globally. As followers of Jesus Christ, each individual Christian is linked to Jesus' compassion for people who are poor and called to work tirelessly on their behalf, as he did.

❶ Include people who are poor and oppressed in your daily prayers.
Keeping the needs of others in mind, especially people who suffer as a result of economic inequality, political oppression, or natural disaster, defines a person's good works. Name specific situations in your prayers, and use specific place names and people's names whenever possible. Keep the newspaper on your lap as you pray, if necessary.

❷ Include people who are poor and oppressed in your personal or household budget.
Dedicate some of your personal giving to economic-aid organizations. This should include your congregation. If you already tithe (give 10 percent of your income to your church), consider earmarking a percentage of that money to go directly to relief organizations through your church's budget.

❸ Pay close attention to economic and political conditions in other nations.

You can't help if you don't know what's really going on. Resolve to be a well-informed person who tests the worldview in the news against the worldview in the Bible. Utilize the Internet to locate independent and alternative news sources with unique, on-the-spot perspectives.

❹ Get to know organizations that work for justice locally.

Your congregation probably already organizes to do justice work in your neighborhood. If not, consider taking responsibility to organize a ministry team in your church.

❺ Make working for justice part of your weekly or monthly routine.

Devote a portion of your time regularly to a specific activity that personally connects you to people who are poor and disenfranchised. There is no substitute for personal contact.

❻ Vote your conscience.

If you are of voting age, remember that nations will be judged by the way they treat people who are disadvantaged. Keep this in mind when you go to your polling place.

❼ Advocate for a cause in which you believe, one that has meaning for you personally.

How to Identify
a Genuine Miracle

The term "miracle" describes something that causes wonder. It is usually used in reference to an event that defies logical explanation and appears to be the work of a higher force, suggesting a reality beyond the five senses.

❶ Disregard most minor situations.
The facts should indicate a situation of high order, such as one that is life-threatening, one involving suffering, or involving an immediate threat. Finding your lost keys does not necessarily constitute a miracle.

❷ Look for a lack of predictability.
A positive outcome should be needed and wanted, but not expected. Miracles tend to occur "out of the blue" rather than as the result of an earthly cause, especially a human one.

❸ Evaluate the outcome.
Miracles achieve a life-giving purpose; they never occur outside the will of God. Suffering is relieved, God is glorified, Jesus' presence is made manifest, the lowly are lifted up, evil is thwarted, creation is revealed, or life is saved. The outcome must be regarded as good, according to biblical standards.

❹ Look for a divine agency.
The ability to make a miracle happen, to guarantee the results, or to take credit for it is beyond human. Often the event will defy what we know to be true about the laws of nature or probability. If anyone stands to make money or advance an agenda from an event, it is most likely not a miracle.

❺ **Adopt a wait-and-see perspective.**
A miracle will still be a miracle later on. Labeling something a miracle too quickly could lead down unhelpful paths, while waiting to make the call — pondering the event in your heart — will enhance your faith journey.

Be Aware

+ The most overlooked miracle is that God shows up in everyday life events and in such ordinary forms as bread, wine, water, words, and people.

+ The miracle of life in Jesus Christ is a daily event and should be regarded as a free gift.

Three Essential Personal Spiritual Rituals

A spiritual ritual is a routine for building one's faith. Ritual involves action, words, and often images that work together to center one's daily life in Jesus Christ. Medical studies show that people who pray regularly throughout the day suffer less stress, have lower incidence of heart disease, and live longer on average than those who do not.

❶ Morning Devotions

+ Directly upon awakening, turn your attention first to God. The silence and solitude available in the morning hours are ideal.

+ Try to make prayer the first activity of your day.

+ If necessary, set your alarm to sound fifteen minutes early to give yourself time.

+ Begin with thanks and by remembering God's constant presence.

+ Identify events you anticipate in your day and how you feel about them.

+ Ask God to provide what you need for the day.

+ Pray on behalf of other people. Consider keeping a list of names tucked inside your Bible or devotional book.

❷ Mealtime Grace

Human beings naturally pause before a meal. Use those moments to give thanks.

- Consider establishing mealtime grace as a household ritual.

- When eating in public, be considerate of others, but do not abandon your ritual.

- Once your meal is assembled and ready to eat, take time before praying to gather your thoughts and call an appropriate prayer to mind.

- Many people pray a rote or memorized prayer at mealtimes. Consider occasionally departing from your regular prayer with an extemporaneous one.

Praying before mealtime is a great personal ritual that can be shared with others.

❸ Evening Prayer

The other daily rituals you perform in the evening, like brushing your teeth or letting the cat out, create a natural structure for evening prayer.

- Establish a regular time, such as sunset or at bedtime, and commit to it.

- Confess wrongdoing and ask for forgiveness.

- Tell God about the joys and sorrows of the day. Ask for help with the sorrows and give thanks for the joys.

- Identify the good things about the day. On bad days, find at least one thing to give thanks for.

- Consider using a devotional as a guide and companion.

- Think about involving other members of your household in this ritual. Evening prayer particularly can be enhanced through sharing. When children are included, trace the cross on their foreheads and say a brief blessing as part of the ritual. (See the illustration on page 103.)

How to Forgive Someone

Forgiving is one of the most difficult disciplines of faith, since it seems to cost you something additional when you've already been wronged. Swallowing your pride and seeking a greater good, however, can yield great healing and growth.

1 Acknowledge that God forgives you.
When you realize that God has already shown forgiveness and continues to forgive sinners like you, it's easier to forgive someone else.

2 Consult Scripture.
Jesus taught the Lord's Prayer to his disciples, who were hungry to become like he was. Forgiveness was a big part of this. Read Matthew 6:9–15.

3 Seek the person out whenever possible.
Consciously decide to deliver your forgiveness in person. In cases where this is geographically impossible, find an appropriate alternative means, such as the telephone. Note: This may not be wise in all cases, given the timing of the situation or the level of hurt. Certain problems can be made worse by an unwelcome declaration of forgiveness. Consult with a clergyperson before taking questionable action.

4 Say, "I forgive you," out loud.
A verbal declaration of forgiveness is ideal. Speaking the words enacts a physical chain reaction that can create healing for both speaker and hearer. In the Bible, Jesus used these words to heal a paralyzed man from across a room.

❺ Pray for the power to forgive.
Praying for this is always good, whether a forgiveness situation is at hand or not. It is especially helpful in cases where declaring forgiveness seems beyond your reach.

Be Aware

• When someone sins against you personally, forgiving them does *not* depend upon them feeling sorry (showing contrition) or asking for your forgiveness. But it helps. You may have to struggle, however, to forgive them without their consent or participation.

How to Confess Your Sins and Receive Forgiveness

Confession is often misunderstood. Think of it less as a self-flagellation and more as a key to unlock the ball and chain represented by the worst part of your past. It's supposed to make you feel free, ready to participate in a whole new world — not tied to guilt and terrified of punishment. It's also sound psychological practice. Any Christian may confess and any Christian may pronounce forgiveness because in the end, forgiveness comes from Jesus Christ himself.

Many UCC congregations practice "corporate confession," in which the whole worshiping body enters into prayer together and confession is made on its behalf by a worship leader. This may include a time of silent prayer for you to add your personal confessions. You might also want to make a private confession by making an appointment with your pastor or sitting down with a good Christian friend. Either way, here are some guidelines.

❶ Make a mental list of your offenses.

❷ Resolve to confess of your own free will.
Don't confess merely because someone else wants you to do it. Make your confession voluntarily.

❸ Make your confession fearlessly, aloud if possible and appropriate.
Confess the sins that burden you, and then confess the sins of which you are not aware or cannot remember. If it's a corporate confession, the person praying will name some possible sins. Own the ones that are yours, and add any not mentioned.

4 **Avoid making up sins.**
More important than the facts and figures is a spirit of repentance in your heart.

5 **Receive forgiveness as it is given, in the name of God.**
God forgives you fully.

6 **Resolve to live joyfully and penitently.**
With absolution comes new life in the freedom of God's grace.

How to Defend Your Faith against Attack

Defending your faith from attack involves tact and savvy, that is, the ability to empathize with your adversary and use his or her affronts creatively without getting baited into an angry or hostile response. Just be ready. There is no substitute for knowing your stuff.

1 **Employ the 80/20 rule.**
In any debate, it is best to listen at least 80 percent of the time and talk 20 percent of the time.

2 **Engage in empathic listening.**
Empathic listening means to try to comprehend not just the content of the other person's position, but also the emotional thrust behind it. This is important especially in cases where the speaker's emotional expressions are intense.

3 **Restate your adversary's argument empathetically.**
Use sentences like, "So, you're upset because Christians seem to say one thing and do another."

4 **Identify with what the speaker is saying.**
For example, say, "I know what you mean. I see a lot of phony behavior at my own church." This elevates the conversation and keeps it civil.

5 **Do your best to put the speaker at ease.**
Having made clear that you understand his or her position, you are free to state your defense or counterpoint. Offer "I statement" responses, such as, "I wonder how I would stand up under that kind of scrutiny, myself," or, "I do my

best not to judge others too harshly. I'd hate to be judged by those standards."

6 **Keep it as upbeat as possible.**
Use humility, humor, and a pleasant nature to defuse any tension. Though hard to practice, it is possible to disagree with someone while remaining friends.

7 **Give your opponent his or her due.**
When the speaker makes a good argument, say, "You make a good point." This will further elevate the conversation. If you still disagree, make your counterargument calmly.

8 **Avoid closing off the conversation or leaving it on a sour note.**
If you can, offer to continue the discussion over a lunch that you buy. Avoid falling into a "winner take all" mind-set. Keep respect as your highest value.

Be Aware

• Attacks on faith are not limited to verbal assaults, especially in places where religious persecution is a reality

• It is best in all cases to avoid sounding smug or preachy where your points resemble counterattacks.

How to Resist Temptation

❶ Run in the opposite direction.
Learn to identify the things that tempt you and avoid situations in which temptation will occur. When you see a temptation coming down the road, take a detour.

❷ Laugh at the tempter.
Temptations are simply things that want to gain power over you. When you laugh at them, you reduce them to their proper place.

❸ Distract yourself with other, healthier activities.
God knows what's good for you and so do you. Find an alternative activity that promotes trust in God and requires you to care for your neighbors. Seek the company of others, especially people to whom you may be of service.

❹ Remember, your Lord also confronted temptation.
Jesus faced down temptation by telling the devil the truth, namely, only God is Lord. Consider using a contemporary version of Jesus' words: "God's in charge here, not you."

❺ Tell the devil to go back to hell.
Consider saying this: "You're right, Mr. Devil. I'm a sinner. Unfortunately, you have no power here. My Lord loves sinners and has forgiven me forever. There's nothing you can do about it. Go back to where you came from and quit bothering me!"

Caution! The following step should be reserved for the rare occasions when the above methods fail and should be attempted only under the counsel of authority.

---

6 **Commit some minor sin to throw the devil off.**
Unchecked temptation often leads to apathy, confusion, and even despair, which is the archenemy of faith. To thwart this process, commit a minor sin to remind yourself that Jesus came specifically to save you from sin. Don't forget to include this sin in your later confession.

Be Aware

• There are different kinds of temptation. Regardless of the type, temptation always involves a hidden voice whispering to you, "Whatever God says, you really need to trust me instead. I'm the only thing that can help you."

• Temptations try to make us trust in ourselves or in other things more than in God. When you realize this, you'll see that everything on the list above is just turning back to Jesus who died to show you how much you can trust him.

Even Jesus faced temptation when the devil confronted him in the wilderness.

How to Care for the Sick

While a trained and licensed physician must be sought to treat illness and injury, there is no malady that cannot be helped with faithful attention and prayer.

1 Assess the nature of the problem.
Visit a local pharmacy if the illness is a simple one. Over-the-counter medications usually provide temporary relief until the body heals itself. If symptoms persist, the sick person should see a doctor and get a more detailed diagnosis.

2 Pray for them.
Intercessory prayers are prayers made on someone else's behalf. Recent studies point to healing in hospitalized patients who have been prayed for — even when the sick persons were not aware of the prayers. Add the afflicted person to your church's prayer list.

3 Call in the elders.
Prayer and emotional support from friends and family are vital parts of healing, living with illness, and facing death. Ask the pastor to assemble the church elders (leaders) for prayer and the laying on of hands.

Here's what the Bible says on this topic: "Are any among you sick? They should call for the elders of the church and have them pray over them, anointing them with oil in the name of the Lord" (James 5:14).

Be Aware

* Many people claim expertise in healing, from acupuncturists and herbalists to "faith healers" and psychics. Use caution and skepticism, but keep an open mind.

* Many people believe that much healing can be found in "comfort foods," such as homemade chicken soup.

* Those who attempt to diagnose and treat their own symptoms can often do more harm than good. When in doubt, always consult a pharmacist, doctor, or other medical professional.

Gather friends, family, and church leaders to pray and lay hands on sick people.

How to Identify and Avoid Evil

The devil delights in unnoticed evil. To this end, the devil employs a wide array of lies, disguises, and deceptions while attacking our relationships with God and each other. A sharp eye and vigilance are your best defense.

❶ Know your enemy.
Evil appears in many forms, most often using camouflage to present itself as kindly or friendly. Cruelty, hatred, violence, and exploitation are among the many forms evil can take, but it often masquerades as justice or something done "for their own good." Be alert to acts, people, and events that employ these methods, even if the eventual outcome appears good.

❷ Proceed carefully and deliberately.
Avoid rushing to conclusions. Use good judgment.

❸ Take action to expose the evil.
Evil relies on darkness. It wants to remain hidden and hates the light of truth. Things that suffer from public knowledge or scrutiny might be evil.

❹ Be prepared to make a personal sacrifice.

Fighting evil can be costly. A successful counterattack may require you to give up something you cherish. For Jesus, as for many of his followers, it was his life. Love is the foundation of sacrifice that combats evil.

❺ Stay vigilant.

Evil's genius is shown in disguise, deception, and misdirection. Maintain your objectivity and apply the biblical measures of right and wrong you know to be correct. A conscience informed by Scripture and common sense is a good standard.

How to Avoid Gossip

Gossip is among the most corrosive forces within a community and should be monitored closely. Discovery of gossip should be viewed as an opportunity to defend your neighbors' integrity, both gossiper and gossipee.

1 Determine whether the conversation at hand qualifies as gossip.

- Gossip involves one party speaking about a second party to a third party.

- The person who is the topic of gossip is not a participant in the conversation.

- The tone of the conversation is often secretive or negative. Gasps and whispers are common.

- The facts expressed in a gossip conversation are often unsubstantiated and have been obtained second- or third-hand.

2 Recall and heed Titus 3:2: "Speak evil of no one."

3 Interject yourself into the conversation politely.
Ask whether the gossipers have spoken directly to the person about whom they are talking. If not, politely ask why. This may give some indication why they are gossiping.

4 Make a statement of fact.
Gossip withers in the face of truth. Make an attempt to parse out what is truly known from conjecture and supposition. State aloud that gossip is disrespectful and unfair.

Avoid gossip. It undermines community and damages relationships.

⑤ Offer an alternative explanation based on fact.
Describe other situations that cast the gossipee in a favorable light. Always try to give people the benefit of the doubt.

Be Aware

• There is a fine line between helping and meddling. Pay close attention to your own motivations and the possible outcomes of your actions.

• Gossip injures both the gossiper and the person who is the subject of rumors.

• Consult the Eighth Commandment.

• For further help, consult James 4:11.

How to Bless Someone

Blessings through history have had many purposes, often involving the passing of wealth or property from one person or generation to another. A Christian blessing is a declaration of the gospel of Jesus Christ to a specific individual — an affirmation that another person is claimed and loved by almighty God. Blessings should be dispensed liberally and with abandon.

❶ Evaluate the need at hand.
People have different needs at different times. When you perceive a need in which a blessing appears appropriate, take time to discern.

❷ Use safe touch.
Human touch is an affirmation with profound physical effects. Healing and emotional release are common. Make sure you use touch that is non-threatening, respectful, and communicates the love of Christ.

❸ Choose an appropriate way to give the blessing.

- Position one or both hands on the person's head. Use a light touch, but one firm enough to let the person know that he or she is being blessed.

- Place one hand on the person's shoulder.

- Trace a cross on the person's forehead.

- Hold both of the person's hands in yours while making good eye contact.

❹ Make a declaration of freedom.

  ◆ Blessings are often most effective when the spoken word is employed. For example: "[insert name here], child of God, you have been sealed by the Holy Spirit and marked with the cross of Christ forever."

  ◆ Consider ad-libbing a verbal blessing that speaks directly to the situation.

  ◆ Whenever possible, include the words spoken at baptism: "In the name of the Father, and of the Son, and of the Holy Spirit."

Be Aware

◆ Indirect blessings are often appropriate. These include but are not limited to favors, prayers, kind words, consolation, a hot meal, shared laughter, and acceptance.

◆ Some cultures consider head-touching impolite or even rude, so always ask permission before making a blessing this way.

Trace the sign of the cross on the person's forehead.

How to Resolve Interpersonal Conflict

Disagreements are part of life. They often occur when we forget that not everyone sees things the same way. Conflict should be viewed as an opportunity to grow, not a contest for domination. UCCers are traditionally shy, but when push comes to shove they value healthy relationships above all.

❶ Adopt a healthy attitude.
Your frame of mind is critical. Approach the situation with forethought and calm. Prayer can be invaluable at this stage. Do not approach the other party when you're angry or upset.

❷ Read Matthew 18:15–20 beforehand.
Consult the Bible to orient your thinking. This is the model Jesus provided and can be used to call to mind an appropriate method.

❸ Talk directly to the person involved.
Avoid "triangulation." Talking about someone to a third party can make the conflict worse, as the person may feel that he or she is the subject of gossip. Speaking with the other person directly eliminates the danger and boosts the odds of a good outcome.

❹ Express yourself without attacking.
Using "I statements" can avoid casting the other person as the "bad guy" and inflaming the conflict. "I statements" are sentences beginning with phrases such as "I feel..." or "I'm uncomfortable when..."

5 **Keep "speaking the truth in love" (Ephesians 4:15) as your goal.**
Your "truth" may not be the other party's. Your objective is to discover and honor each other's "truth," not to put down the other person. Be ready to admit your own faults and mistakes.

6 **Seek out a third party to act as an impartial witness.**
If direct conversation doesn't resolve the conflict, locate someone both parties trust to sit in. This can help clarify your positions and bring understanding.

7 **Build toward forgiveness and a renewed friendship.**
Agree upon how you will communicate to prevent future misunderstandings.

Be Aware

+ Seemingly unrelated events in your or the other person's life may be playing an invisible role in the conflict at hand. Be ready to shift the focus to the real cause.

+ You may not be able to resolve the conflict at this time, but don't give up on future opportunities.

When two people aren't getting long, sometimes an impartial third person can help resolve the dispute.

How to Console Someone

Consolation is a gift from God. Christians in turn give it to others to build up the body of Christ and preserve it in times of trouble (see 2 Corinthians 1:4–7). UCCers often employ food as a helpful secondary means.

❶ Listen first.
Make it known that you're present and available. When the person opens up, be quiet and attentive.

❷ Be ready to help the person face grief and sadness, not avoid them.
The object is to help the person name, understand, and work through his or her feelings, not gloss over them.

❸ Avoid saying things to make yourself feel better.
"I know exactly how you feel" is seldom true and trivializes the sufferer's pain. Even if you have experienced something similar, no experience is exactly the same. If there is nothing to say, simply be present with the person.

❹ Show respect with honesty.
Don't try to answer the mysteries of the universe or force your beliefs on the person. Be clear about the limitations of your abilities. Be ready to let some questions go unanswered. Consolation isn't about having all the answers; it's about bearing one another's burdens.

❺ Don't put words in God's mouth.
Avoid saying, "This is God's will" or, "This is part of God's plan." Unless you heard it straight from God, don't say it.

How to Cope
with Loss and Grief

Some of us tend to downplay our losses by saying, "Well, it could be worse." This may provide only temporary relief at best. Any loss can cause pain, feelings of confusion, and uncertainty. These responses are normal.

❶ Familiarize yourself with the stages of grief.
Experts identify five: denial, anger, bargaining, depression, and acceptance. Some add hope as a sixth stage. Grieving persons cycle back and forth through the stages, sometimes experiencing two or three in a single day. This is normal.

❷ Express your grief.
Healthy ways may include crying, staring into space for extended periods, ruminating, shouting at the ceiling, and sudden napping. Laughing outbursts are also appropriate and should not be judged harshly.

❸ Identify someone you trust to talk to.
Available people can include a spouse, parents, relatives, friends, a pastor, a doctor, or a trained counselor. Many household pets also make good listeners and willing confidants.

❹ Choose a personal way to memorialize the loss.
Make a collage of photographs, offer a memorial donation to your church, or start a scrapbook of memories to honor the event. This helps you to begin to heal without getting stuck in your grief.

Be Aware

+ Many experts prescribe a self-giving activity, such as volunteering at a shelter or soup kitchen, as a means of facilitating a healty grieving process.

+ The pain immediately after suffering a loss is usually deep and intense. This will lessen with the passage of time.

+ Anger, guilt, bitterness, and sadness are likely emotions.

+ Short-term depression may occur in extreme cases. After experiencing a great loss, such as the death of a loved one, make an appointment with your family physician for a physical.

+ Even Jesus cried when his friend Lazarus died (John 11:35).

Even Jesus felt the loss of Lazarus when he died.

Mary   Martha

The Top Ten Attributes
to Look For in a Spouse/Partner

While no single personality trait can predict a compatible marriage, the following list frames the basic things to look for in a spouse. With all attributes, some differences can be the source of a couple's strength rather than a source of difficulty. Statistically, UCCers appear to be about as successful at choosing a spouse/partner as other people.

❶ Similar values.
Values that concern religion beliefs, life purposes, financial priorities, and children are a foundation on which to build the relationship. Contrary values tend to create discord.

❷ Physical-energy and physical-space compatibility.
Consider whether the person's energy level and physical-space needs work with yours. Also, the word "compatibility" can mean a complementary match of opposites, or it can denote a match based on strong similarities.

❸ Physical and romantic compatibility.
If the two of you have a similar degree of interest in or need for physical and romantic expression in your relationship, the chance of lifelong compatibility increases.

❹ Intellectual parity.
Communicating with someone who has a significantly different intelligence level or educational background can require extra effort.

⑤ Emotional maturity.
A lifelong relationship of mutual challenge and support often helps each person grow emotionally, but a lifetime spent waiting for someone to grow up could be more frustration than it's worth.

⑥ Sense of humor.
Sense of humor can provide an excellent measure of a person's personality and an important means to couple survival. If he or she doesn't get your jokes, you could be asking for trouble.

⑦ Respect.
Look for someone who listens to you without trying to control you. Look also for a healthy sense of self-respect.

⑧ Trustworthiness.
Seek out someone who is honest and acts with your best interests in mind — not only his or hers — and tries to learn from his or her mistakes.

⑨ Forgiving.
When you sincerely apologize to your spouse, he or she should try to work through and get beyond the problem rather than hold on to it. Once forgiven, past mistakes should not be raised, especially in conflict situations.

⑩ Kindness.
An attitude of consistent kindness may be the most critical attribute for a lifelong partnership.

Be Aware

- If you live to be old, you will probably experience major changes that you cannot predict at age fifteen or twenty-five or thirty-five. Accepting this fact in advance can help you weather difficult times.

- Use all of your resources — intuition, emotions, and rational thought — to make the decision about a life partner.

- Family members and trusted friends can offer invaluable advice in this decision-making process and should be consulted.

How to Banish the Devil from Your Presence

Bodily acts hold the power to send the devil packing. While the existence of a "person" devil — a physical entity embodying pure evil — is part of the Christian tradition, UCCers tend to withhold final judgment on specifics. Still, it's good to be prepared.

❶ Laugh out loud.
Laughter is abhorrent to the devil and should be indulged in frequently.

❷ Make the sign of the cross.
The devil hates the cross because that is where God's love for you is most evident.

❸ Seek the company of other believers.
Play games with children, attend worship, join a prayer team, host a dinner party, or locate a Bible study. Solitude can provide the devil an opportunity.

❹ Serve those who have less than you.
Resolve to volunteer your time to help those less fortunate than you. The devil is thwarted by the love of Christ in action.

❺ Confess your sins.
The devil is attracted to a guilty conscience. Confession clears the conscience and emboldens the believer.

6 **Break wind.**
The devil (along with anyone else in the room) might well leave you alone. You can thank Martin Luther for this suggestion; it was one of his favorites.

7 **Consider what you might be doing to invite the devil into your life.**
We invite the devil into our lives when our actions and values no longer center on Christ.

Banish the devil by taking part in activities with others.
Avoid excessive solitude.

How to Be Saved
(by Grace through Faith
and Not by Your Good Works)

Many religions are built on the idea that the more closely people follow the religious rules or the more morally people behave, the better God will like them — and the better God likes them, the greater their chances of "getting into heaven."

While there is nothing wrong with moral living or obeying God's laws, that kind of behavior has very little to do with the salvation God offers. You don't need to be a follower of Jesus Christ for that.

Christianity, on the other hand, says that out of pure love God was willing to sacrifice everything — even his only Son — to save you forever from sin, death, and all your false gods. Including you.

Since God has already done everything needed to secure your salvation through Jesus, you never have to do one single thing to earn God's favor, no matter how bad you are at following the rules. Still, being saved takes some getting used to.

❶ Get familiar with the word "grace."
Grace means that God gives you all the good stuff — forgiveness, salvation, love, and life, with all its ups and downs — as totally free gifts. Keep an eye out for situations in which you can use this word, and then use it liberally. You'll soon begin to see God's grace all around you.

② Practice letting go of things you love.
Staying focused on yourself can make it difficult to open up to a grace-filled world. But giving of yourself, your time and your possessions can put you in a receptive, open frame of mind. This is important, as salvation cannot be "found" by looking for it; it is only revealed.

③ Lose yourself as often as possible.
An important part of having a receptive frame of mind is losing yourself in whatever you're doing. To do this, give yourself over entirely to the activity. This can be accomplished in prayer and worship, but also through things like playing games, talking with friends and family, reading a good book, serving others, or playing a musical instrument. Even work can accomplish this.

④ Admit your limitations.
Without straying into despair or false modesty, make an honest confession to yourself about what you can and cannot do, what you are and what you are not. When you see yourself realistically you become more open to God's message of love, grace, and salvation.

⑤ Accept your uniqueness.
When you accept that to God you are priceless beyond imagining it becomes easier to understand why God chose to save you.

⑥ Spend time in worship and prayer to the living God.
While only God grants the faith that saves, the church gives lots of opportunities where God has promised to come to you.

❼ Avoid the temptation to "do."

The "old Adam" or "old Eve" in you — the sinner in you — always wants to be in charge over God. He or she will tell you that God's grace is too good to be true and that you must "do" something to earn or justify it. Simply remind him or her that you were baptized into Jesus Christ and have all the grace you need.

Be Aware

+ The Apostle Paul's summary of the gospel goes like this: "For by grace you have been saved through faith, and this is not your own doing; it is the gift of God — not the result of works, so that no one may boast" (Ephesians 2:8–9).

+ This viewpoint about God's grace, even among many Christians, is unpopular, as it was when reformers reminded the church of it almost five hundred years ago. Be aware that once you adopt it you will come under fire and be tempted to lapse back into the old way.

GRACE

Getting familiar with this very important word
will help you get used to being saved.

How to Reform the Church When It Strays from the Gospel

To stay faithful to the gospel, the church still depends on all its members to call it back, not to their own personal visions, but to Jesus' vision.

① Know your stuff.
You can't call the church back to the gospel if you don't learn for yourself what the gospel is. Read your Bible regularly. Also, spend time in conversation with good theologians, like pastors and church elders.

② Trust your conscience, but equip it first with good information.
To defy corrupt church authorities, draw strength from even more powerful sources, your faith in God and your conscience.

③ Double-check and triple-check your motivations. Are you fighting on behalf of the gospel or for your own personal agenda?
Knowing the difference between the two matters. Some things may be worthy social causes that deserve your time and attention, but they may not be the gospel.

④ Speak out. Act.
It isn't enough just to take a stand or hold an opinion. Once you're sure you're doing it for the right reasons, find an effective way to make change happen.

❺ Prepare to defend yourself, and your message of reform, from attack.

People tend to dislike reform — and institutions like it even less. While the church calls us to model the love of Christ and live by his teachings, sometimes the church and its leaders respond to reformers with a "kill the messenger" attitude.

❻ Keep steady, be patient, and listen to wise counsel.

The Reformation took decades to take root. During that time, reformers battled church authorities. They also debated with each other about the best way to bring the gospel to a new age and restore the church to its real purpose.

How to Tell a Sinner from Saint

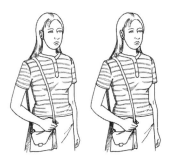

It's impossible to tell a sinner from a saint,
because all people are fully both.
The church is filled with them.

How to Encounter the Holy Trinity as One God in Three Persons

The Trinity is a mystery. Even great theologians don't completely understand, and some scholars spend their whole lives studying it. After two thousand years Christians still believe in this mystery because it gives life and shape to everything in our lives — our relationships, our faith, and especially our worship.

❶ Get to know the three Trinitarian creeds: the Nicene Creed, the Athanasian Creed, and the Apostle's Creed. Consider memorizing each one (two of them are pretty long).
These three testimonies of faith, as they are sometimes called, were written during different times of crisis when clear statements about what Christians believed were needed. While different from each other, they each teach a lot about the three-personed God.

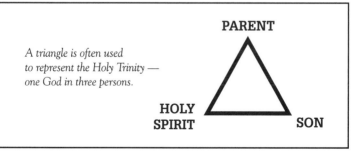

A triangle is often used to represent the Holy Trinity — one God in three persons.

PARENT

HOLY SPIRIT

SON

2 **Include the sign of the cross and the baptismal words as a regular part of your prayer life and worship life.**
The sign if the cross goes with the words, "In the name of the Father (or Parent, or Father-Mother), and of the Son, and of the Holy Spirit," which traces a physical reminder of the Trinity on your body.

3 **Understand that you were made in God's image.**
Just as the one God is Parent, Son, and Holy Spirit all at once, you are mind, body, and soul all at once. Because you reflect the image of God, you were made to live a life of worship in which everything you do and say honors her.

4 **Spend time in the community of faith.**
Go to worship, fellowship, Bible study, Sunday school, and anything else that regularly keeps you in the company of other Christians.

5 **Seek out God's Word and the means of grace.**
The Trinity is revealed in reading the Bible, preaching, the sacraments, the forgiveness of sins, the community of believers, and within anything else where Jesus, the living Word, is active.

Be Aware

• Some people use handy metaphors to begin to get a handle on the doctrine of the Trinity. For example, water takes three major forms: liquid, solid, and gas. Yet it remains one substance. Such metaphors are very useful to a point, but ultimately they must give way to the divine mystery that remains.

Testimonies, Not Tests

To join a United Church of Christ congregation, you do not need to be able to put a check mark next to each entry in some list of fundamental beliefs or truths. You *do* need to be willing to covenant, or promise, to act in certain ways with your congregation. These promises vary from church to church, but will include things like: worshiping together, serving each other and the world, seeking truth together, giving your resources, and more. Think of it like a marriage, only with a hundred times the chores, a thousand times the in-laws — and ten thousand times the love and support.

Which is not to say that we don't have any idea what to believe. One of the best attempts to put it on paper is the Statement of Faith on the following page.

United Church of Christ Statement of Faith: Some Things We Strongly Hope You Might Consider Believing

We believe in you, O God, Eternal Spirit, God of our Savior Jesus Christ and our God, and to your deeds we testify:

You call the worlds into being, create persons in your own image, and set before each one the ways of life and death.

You seek in holy love to save all people from aimlessness and sin.

You judge people and nations by your righteous will declared through prophets and apostles.

In Jesus Christ, the man of Nazareth, our crucified and risen Savior, you have come to us and shared our common lot, conquering sin and death and reconciling the world to yourself.

You bestow upon us your Holy Spirit, creating and renewing the church of Jesus Christ, binding in covenant faithful people of all ages, tongues, and races.

You call us into your church to accept the cost and joy of discipleship, to be your servants in the service of others, to proclaim the gospel to all the world and resist the powers of evil, to share in Christ's baptism and eat at his table, to join him in his passion and victory.

You promise to all who trust you forgiveness of sins and fullness of grace, courage in the struggle for justice and peace, your presence in trial and rejoicing, and eternal life in your realm which has no end.

Blessing and honor, glory and power be unto you.

Amen.

Hey, Who You Calling Autonomous?

The UCC is all about congregational autonomy. Each local church, or congregation, is free from the control of other settings of the church, including the national setting, conferences, associations, and other congregations. And as if that weren't enough, not only are congregations autonomous, so are all the other parts: associations, conferences, schools and seminaries, and the national setting. Notice we said free from "control," not relationship; we listen carefully to each other and hang together even when we don't agree.

Each congregation:

+ Decides how to worship, including how communion is done, whom to baptize or marry, what hymnal to use, what kind of music to have, whether to sin, trespass, or debt in the Lord's Prayer, and more.

+ Decides whether and what to proclaim on theological matters from original sin to the Second Coming.

+ Decides what stands, if any, to take on cultural issues of the day such as war and peace, justice issues, homosexuality, abortion, and more.

+ Decides how to spend its money — including whether to share any with the rest of us. (See "Show Me the Money," page 188.)

+ Hires and fires its own pastors. Other parts of the denomination can help with this, but in the end it's all up to your search committee, the Holy Spirit, and a congregational vote.

- Owns and is responsible for its own property. A mixed blessing: on the one hand, nobody can threaten to take the church building away if we don't behave; on the other, nobody but you and the lady in the pew next to you is going to pay to fix that priceless stained-glass window the youth group hit a softball through.

Sound like a recipe for chaos? It is. But the idea is that each congregation isn't so much making its own decisions as it is making *Christ's* decisions (See "Are You There, God? It's Me, Church," page 190). We have learned to trust that God is at work even in churches that do things that seem strange or ridiculous to us (for instance, see "Ten Firsts of the UCC," page 180). So we stay in covenant (or "promise") relationship with each other, listening, learning, and agreeing or disagreeing respectfully.

Even if it sometimes looks like chaos to us, it's all part of a pattern of God's making.

Bible Stuff

Written down by many people over hundreds of years, the Bible is more like a portable bookshelf than one book by itself. And because the Bible is God's Word, people often feel overwhelmed when they try to read it. This section includes:

+ Helpful information about when, where, and why people wrote the sixty-six books in the Bible. (It didn't all come together at once.)

+ Tips for reading and understanding the Bible — how it's organized and what it says.

+ Some of the most mystifying, hair-raising, and just plain off-the-wall stories in the Bible.

Common Translations of the Bible

Translation	Grade Level*	Theological Affiliation	Year Released	Special Features
King James Version	12.0	Church of England, conservative and evangelical	1611	Poetic style using Elizabethan English. Most widely used translation for centuries.
New American Standard Bible	11.0	Conservative and evangelical	1971; updated, 1995	Revision of the 1901 American Standard Version into contemporary language.
New Revised Standard Version	8.1	Mainline and interconfessional	1989	Updated version of the Revised Standard Version.
New King James Version	8.0	Transnational, transdenominational, conservative, and evangelical	1982	Updates the King James text into contemporary language.
New International Version	7.8	Transnational, transdenominational, conservative, and evangelical	1978; revised, 1984	Popular modern-language version. Attempts to balance literal and dynamic translation methods.
Today's English Version (also called the ~~ ~~ ~~)	7.3	Evangelical and interconfessional	1976	Noted for its freshness of language.

Version	Grade level*	Tradition	Date	Description
New American Bible	6.6	Roman Catholic	1970; revised NT, 1986; revised Psalms, 1991	Official translation of the Roman Catholic Church in the United States.
New Living Translation	6.4	Evangelical	1996	A meaning-for-meaning translation. Successor to the Living Bible.
New Century Version	5.6	Conservative and evangelical	1988; revised, 1991	Follows the *Living Word Vocabulary*.
Contemporary English Version	5.4	Conservative, evangelical, mainline	1995	Easy-to-read English for new Bible readers.
The Message	4.8, from NT samples	Evangelical	2002	An expressive paraphrase of the Bible.

*The grade level on which the text is written, using Dale-chall, Fry, Raygor, and Spache Formulas.

Bible classifications

Apocrypha Bible: Contains certain books that Protestants don't consider canonical. Most of these OT books are accepted by the Roman Catholic Church.

Children's Bible: Includes illustrations and other study aids that are especially helpful for children.

Concordance Bible: Lists places in the Bible where key words are found.

Red Letter Bible: The words spoken by Christ appear in red.

Reference Bible: Pages include references to other Bible passages on the same subject.

Self-Proclaiming Bible: Diacritical marks (as in a dictionary) appear above difficult names and words to help with the pronunciation.

Text Bible: Contains text without footnotes or column references. May include maps, illustrations, and other helpful material.

Sixty Essential Bible Stories

	Story	Bible Text	Key Verse
1.	Creation	Genesis 1-2	Genesis 1:27
2.	The Human Condition	Genesis 3-4	Genesis 3:5
3.	The Flood and the First Covenant	Genesis 6-9	Genesis 9:8
4.	The Tower of Babel and Abraham and Sarah	Genesis 11-12	Genesis 12:1
5.	Sarah, Hagar, and Abraham	Genesis 12-25	Genesis 17:19
6.	Isaac and Rebecca	Genesis 22-25	Genesis 24:67
7.	Jacob and Esau	Genesis 25-36	Genesis 28:15
8.	Joseph and God's Hidden Ways	Genesis 37-50	Genesis 50:20
9.	Moses and Pharaoh	Exodus 1-15	Exodus 2:23
10.	The Ten Commandments	Exodus 20	Exodus 20:2
11.	From the Wilderness into the Promised Land	Exodus 16-18; Deuteronomy 1-6; Joshua 1-3, 24	Deuteronomy 6:4
12.	Judges	Book of Judges	Judges 21:25
13.	Ruth	Book of Ruth	Ruth 4:14
14.	Samuel and Saul	1 Samuel 1-11	1 Samuel 3:1
15.	King David	multiple OT books	1 Samuel 8:6
16.	David, Nathan, and What Is a Prophet?	2 Samuel 11-12	2 Samuel 7:12
17.	Solomon	1 Kings 1-11	1 Kings 6:12
18.	Split of the Kingdom	1 Kings 11ff	1 Kings 12:16
19.	Northern Kingdom, Its Prophets and Fate	1 Kings—2 Kings 17	Amos 5:21
20.	Southern Kingdom, Its Prophets and Fate (Part 1)	multiple OT books	Isaiah 5:7

Sixty Essential Bible Stories

	Story	Bible Text	Key Verse
21.	Southern Kingdom, Its Prophets and Fate (Part 2)	multiple OT books	Jeremiah 31:31
22.	The Exile	Isaiah 40-55; Ezekiel	Isaiah 40:10
23.	Return from Exile	multiple OT books	Ezra 1:1
24.	Ezra and Nehemiah	Books of Ezra and Nehemiah	Ezra 3:10
25.	Esther	Book of Esther	Esther 4:14
26.	Job	Book of Job	Job 1:1
27.	Daniel	Book of Daniel	Daniel 3:17
28.	Psalms of Praise and Trust	Psalms 8, 30, 100, 113, 121	Psalm 121:1
29.	Psalms for Help	various psalms	Psalm 22:1
30.	Wisdom	Job, Proverbs, Ecclesiastes	Proverbs 1:7
31.	The Annunciation	Luke 1:26-56	Luke 1:31-33
32.	Magi	Matthew 2:1-12	Matthew 2:2-3
33.	Birth of Jesus	Luke 2:1-20	Luke 2:10-11
34.	Simeon	Luke 2:25-35	Luke 2:30-32
35.	Wilderness Temptations	Matthew 4:1-11; Mark 1:12-13; Luke 4:1-13	Luke 4:12-13
36.	Jesus' Nazareth Sermon	Matthew 13:54-58; Mark 6:1-6: Luke 4:16-30	Luke 4:18-19, 21
37.	Jesus Calls the First Disciples	Matthew 4:18-22; Mark 1:16-20; Luke 5:1-11	Luke 5:9-10
38.	Beatitudes	Matthew 5:3-12	Luke 6:20-26
39.	Gerasene Demoniac	Matthew 8:28-34; Mark 5:1-20; Luke 8:26-39	Luke 8:39
40.	Feeding of the 5,000	Matthew 14:13-21; Mark 6:30-44; Luke 9:10-17; John 6:1-14	Luke 9:16-17

Sixty Essential Bible Stories

	Story	Bible Text	Key Verse
41.	The Transfguration	Matthew 17:1-8; Mark 9:2-8: Luke 9:28-36	Luke 9:34-35
42.	Sending of the Seventy	Matthew 8:19-22; Luke 10:1-16	Luke 10:8, 16
43.	Good Samaritan	Luke 10:25-37	Luke 10:27-28
44.	Healing the Bent-Over Woman	Luke 13:10-17	Luke 13:16
45.	Parables of Lost and Found	Luke 15:1-32	Luke 15:31-32
46.	Rich Man and Lazarus	Luke 16:19-31	Luke 16:29-31
47.	Zacchaeus	Luke 19:1-11	Luke 19:9
48.	Sheep and Goats	Matthew 25:31-46	Matthew 25:40
49.	Parable of the Vineyard	Matthew 21:33-46; Mark 12:1-12; Luke 20:9-19; (Isaiah 5:1-7)	Luke 20:14-16
50.	The Last Supper	Matthew 26:20-29; Mark 14:12-16: Luke 22:14-38	Luke 22:19-20, 27
51.	Crucifxion	Matthew 27; Mark 15; Luke 23; John 19	Luke 23:42-43, 46
52.	Road to Emmaus	Luke 24	Luke 24:30-31
53.	Pentecost	Acts 2:1-21	Acts 2:17-18
54.	Healing the Lame Man	Acts 3-4	Acts 4:19
55.	Baptism of the Ethiopian	Acts 8:26-39	Acts 8:35-37
56.	Call of Saul	Acts 7:58—8:1, 9:1-30	Acts 9:15-16
57.	Peter and Cornelius	Acts 10	Acts 10:34-35
58.	Philippians Humility	Philippians 2:1-13	Philippians 2:12-13
59.	Love Hymn	1 Corinthians 13	1 Corinthians 13:4-7
60.	Resurrection	1 Corinthians 15	1 Corinthians 15:51-55

How to Read the Bible

The Bible is a collection of sixty separate books gathered together over hundreds of years and thousands of miles. Divided into the Old Testament (Hebrew language) and the New Testament (Greek language), these writings have many authors and take many forms.

The Bible includes histories, stories, prophecies, poetry, songs, teachings, and laws, to name a few. Christians believe the Bible is the story of God's relationship with humankind and a powerful way that God speaks to people.

❶ Determine your purpose for reading.
Clarify in your own mind what you hope to gain. Your motivations should be well intentioned, such as to seek information, to gain a deeper understanding of God and yourself, or to enrich your faith. Pray for insight before every reading time.

❷ Resolve to read daily.
Commit to a daily regimen of Bible reading. Make it a part of your routine until it becomes an unbreakable habit.

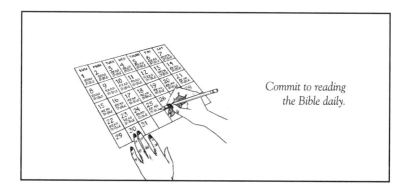

*Commit to reading
the Bible daily.*

❸ Master the mechanics.

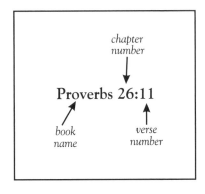

- Memorize the books of the Bible in order.

- Familiarize yourself with the introductory material. Many Bible translations include helpful information at the front of the Bible and at the beginning of each book.

- The books are broken down into chapters and verses. Locate the beginning of a book by using the Bible's table of contents. Follow the numerical chapter numbers; these are usually in large type. Verses are likewise numbered in order within each chapter. Simply run your finger down the page until you locate the verse number you're looking for.

- If your Bible contains maps (usually in the back), consult them when cities, mountains, or seas are mentioned in your reading.

❹ Befriend the written text.
Read with a pen or pencil in hand and underline passages of interest. Look up unfamiliar words in a dictionary. Write notes in the margins when necessary. The Bible was written to be read and used, not worshiped.

❺ Practice reading from the Bible out loud.

❻ Read With a Group.
Support, question, and challenge one another as you go.

How to Memorize
a Bible Verse

Memorizing Scripture is an ancient faith practice. Its value is often mentioned by people who have, in crisis situations, remembered comforting or reassuring passages coming to mind, sometimes decades after first memorizing them. There are three common methods of memorization.

Method 1:
Memorize with Music

Choose a verse that is special for you. It is more difficult to remember something that doesn't make sense to you or that lacks meaning.

1 **Choose a familiar tune.**
Pick something catchy and repetitious.

2 **Add the words from the Bible verse to your tune.**
Mix up the words a bit, if necessary. Memorizing a verse "word for word" isn't always as important as learning the message of the verse.

3 **Mark the verse in your Bible.**
This will help you find it again later on. Consider highlighting or underlining it.

4 **Make the words rhyme, if possible.**

Method 2:
The Three S's:
See It, Say It, Script It

This method works on the principle of multisensory reinforcement. The brain creates many more neural pathways to a memory through sight, speech, and manipulation (writing) than just one of these, so recall is quicker and easier.

❶ Write the verse on index cards in large print.
Post the cards in places you regularly look, such as the refrigerator door or bathroom mirror.

❷ Say the verse out loud.
Repeat the verse ten times to yourself every time you notice one of your index cards.

❸ Write the verse down.

❹ Try saying and writing the verse at the same time.
Repeat.

Write the verse out
longhand several
dozen times.

Method 3:
Old-Fashioned Memorization

Attempt this method only if you consider yourself to be "old school" or if the other methods fail.

❶ Write the verse out by hand on paper.
A whiteboard can work extremely well, also. Consider writing it as many as a hundred times. Repeat this process until you can recite the verse flawlessly.

❷ Don't get up until you've memorized the verse.
Open your Bible to the appropriate verse, sit down in front of it, and don't get up, eat, sleep, or use the bathroom until you can recite it flawlessly.

❸ Enlist a family member or friend to help you.
Have them read along with you and prompt you when you get stuck.

The Top Ten Bible Villains

❶ Satan

The Evil One is known by many names in the Bible and appears in many places, but the devil's purpose is always the same: to disrupt and confuse people so that they turn from God and seek to become their own gods. This Bible villain is still active today.

❷ The Serpent

In Eden the serpent succeeded in tempting Eve to eat from the tree of the knowledge of good and evil (Genesis 3:1–7). As a result, sin entered creation. If it weren't for the serpent, we'd all still be walking around naked, eating fresh fruit, and living forever.

❸ Pharaoh (probably Seti I or Rameses II)

The notorious Pharaoh from the book of Exodus enslaved the Israelites. Moses eventually begged him to "let my people go," but Pharaoh hardened his heart and refused. Ten nasty plagues later, Pharaoh relented, but then changed his mind again. In the end, with his army at the bottom of the sea, Pharaoh finally gave his slaves up to the wilderness.

❹ Goliath

"The Philistine of Gath," who stood six cubits in height (about nine feet tall), was sent to fight David, still a downy-headed youth of fifteen. Goliath was a fighting champion known for killing people, but David drilled Goliath in the head with a rock from his sling and gave God the glory (1 Samuel 17).

one
cubit

Though physically powerful, Goliath lost his battle with young David, one of the Top Ten heroes of the Bible.

Goliath   David

⑤ Jezebel

King Ahab of Judah's wife and a follower of the false god Baal, Jezebel led her husband away from God and tried to kill off the prophets of the Lord. Elijah the prophet, however, was on the scene. He shamed Jezebel's false prophets and killed them (1 Kings 18:40).

⑥ King Herod

Afraid of any potential threat to his power, upon hearing about the birth of the Messiah in Bethlehem Herod sent the Wise Men to pinpoint his location. Awestruck by the Savior in the cradle, the Wise Men went home by a different route and avoided Herod. In a rage, he ordered the murder of every child two years of age or younger in the vicinity of Bethlehem. The baby Messiah escaped with his parents to Egypt (Matthew 2:14–15).

❼ The Pharisees, Sadducees, and Scribes
They dogged Jesus throughout his ministry, alternately challenging his authority and being awed by his power. It was their leadership, with the consent and blessing of the people and the Roman government, that brought Jesus to trial and execution.

❽ Judas
One of Jesus' original disciples, Judas earned thirty pieces of silver by handing his Lord over to the authorities. He accomplished this betrayal by leading the soldiers into the garden of Gethsemane, where he identified Jesus with a kiss (Matthew 26–27).

❾ Pontius Pilate
The consummate politician, the Roman governor chose to preserve his own bloated status by giving the people what they wanted: Jesus' crucifixion. He washed his hands to signify self-absolution, but bloodied them instead.

❿ God's People
They whine, they sin, they turn their backs on God over and over again. When given freedom, they blow it. When preached repentance by God's prophets, they stone them. When offered a Savior, we kill him. In the end, it must be admitted, God's people — us! — don't really shine. Only by God's grace and the gift of faith in Jesus Christ do we have hope.

The Top Ten Bible Heroes

The Bible is filled with typical examples of heroism, but another kind of hero inhabits the pages of the Bible — those people who, against all odds, follow God no matter the outcome. These are heroes of faith.

❶ Noah

In the face of ridicule from others, Noah trusted God when God chose him to build an ark to save a remnant of humanity from destruction. Noah's trust became part of a covenant with God.

Noah trusted God, even though others made fun of him. By following God's instructions and building a great ark, Noah and his family survived the flood (Genesis 6–10).

❷ Abraham and Sarah

In extreme old age, Abraham and Sarah answered God's call to leave their home and travel to a strange land, where they became the parents of God's people.

❸ Moses

Moses, a man with a speech impediment, challenged the Egyptian powers to deliver God's people from bondage. He led a rebellious and contrary people for forty years through the wilderness and gave them God's law.

❹ Rahab

A prostitute who helped Israel conquer the promised land, Rahab was the great-grandmother of King David, and thus a part of the family of Jesus himself.

❺ David

Great King David, the youngest and smallest member of his family, defeated great enemies, turning Israel into a world power. He wrote psalms, led armies, and confessed his sins to the Lord.

❻ Mary and Joseph

These humble peasants responded to God's call to be the parents of the Messiah, although the call came through a pregnancy that was not the result of marriage.

❼ The Canaanite Woman

Desperate for her daughter's health, the Canaanite woman challenged Jesus regarding women and race by claiming God's love for all people (Matthew 15:21–28). Because of this, Jesus praised her faith.

8 Peter

Peter was a man quick to speak but slow to think. At Jesus' trial, Peter denied ever having known him. But in the power of forgiveness and through Christ's appointment, Peter became a leader in the early church.

9 Saul/Paul

Originally an enemy and persecutor of Christians, Paul experienced a powerful vision of Jesus, converted, and became the greatest missionary the church has ever known.

10 Phoebe

A contemporary of Paul's, Phoebe is believed to have delivered the book of Romans after traveling some eight hundred miles from Cenchrea near Corinth to Rome. A wealthy woman, she used her influence to travel, to protect other believers, and to host worship services in her home.

Phoebe is believed to have delivered the book of Romans after traveling eight hundred miles.

The Three Most Rebellious Things Jesus Did

❶ The prophet returned to his hometown (Luke 4:14–27).
Jesus returned to Nazareth, where he was raised and was invited to read Scripture and preach. First, he insisted that the Scriptures he read were not just comforting promises of a distant future, but that they were about him, local boy, anointed by God. Second, he insisted God would bless foreigners with those same promises through him. These statements amounted to the unpardonable crime of blasphemy!

❷ The rebel thumbed his nose at the authorities (John 11:55–12:11).
Jesus had become an outlaw, hunted by the religious authorities who wanted to kill him. Mary, Martha, and Lazarus threw a thank-you party for Jesus in Bethany, right outside Jerusalem, the authorities' stronghold. In spite of the threats to his life, Jesus went to the party. This was not just rebellion but a demonstration of how much Jesus loved his friends.

❸ The king rode a royal procession right under Caesar's nose (Matthew 21:1–17; Mark 11:1–10; Luke 19:28–38; John 12:12–19).
Jesus entered Jerusalem during a great festival, in full view of adoring crowds, as a king come home to rule. Riding the colt, heralded by the people with cloaks and branches, accompanied by the royal anthem (Psalm 118), he rode in to claim Jerusalem for God and himself as God's anointed. The Roman overlords and the Jewish leaders watched this seditious act and prepared for a crucifixion.

The Seven Funniest Bible Stories

Humor isn't scarce in the Bible; you just have to look for it. For example, God tells Abraham (a hundred years old) and Sarah (in her nineties) that they'll soon have a son. Understandably, they laugh. Later, they have a son named Isaac, which means "he laughs." Bible humor is also ironic, gross, and sometimes just plain bizarre.

1 **Gideon's dog-men (Judges 6:11–7:23).**
God chooses Gideon to lead an army against the Midianites. Gideon gathers an army of thirty-two thousand, men, but this is too many. God tells Gideon to make all the men drink from a stream, and then selects only the three hundred men who lap water like dogs.

2 **David ambushes Saul in a cave while he's "busy" (1 Samuel 24:2–7).**
While pursuing David cross-country to engage him in battle, Saul goes into a cave to "relieve himself" (move his bowels). Unbeknownst to Saul, David and his men are already hiding in the very same cave. While Saul's doing his business, David sneaks up and cuts off a corner of Saul's cloak with a knife. Outside afterward, David shows King Saul the piece of cloth to prove he could have killed him "on the throne."

3 **King David busts a move (2 Samuel 12–23).**
David is so excited about bringing the Ark of the Covenant to Jerusalem that he dances before God and all the people dressed only in a linen ephod, an apron-like garment that covered only the front of his body.

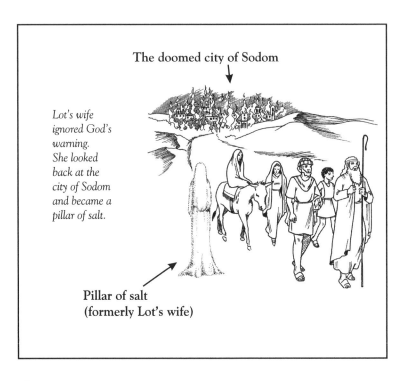

The doomed city of Sodom

Lot's wife ignored God's warning. She looked back at the city of Sodom and became a pillar of salt.

Pillar of salt
(formerly Lot's wife)

4 Lot's wife (Genesis 19:24–26).

While fleeing God's wrath upon the cities of Sodom and Gomorrah, Lot's wife forgets (or ignores) God's warning not to look back upon the destruction and turns into a woman-sized pillar of salt.

5 Gerasene demoniac (Mark 5:1–20).

A man is possessed by so many demons that chains cannot hold him. Jesus exorcises the demons and sends them into a herd of two thousand pigs, which then run over the edge of a cliff and drown in the sea. The herders, now two thousand pigs poorer, get miffed and ask Jesus to leave.

6 Disciples and loaves of bread (Mark 8:14–21).
The disciples were there when Jesus fed five thousand people with just five loaves of bread and two fish. They also saw him feed four thousand people with seven loaves. Later, in a boat, the disciples fret to an exasperated Jesus because they have only one loaf for thirteen people.

7 Peter can't swim (Matthew 14:22–33).
Blundering Peter sees Jesus walking on the water and wants to join him. But when the wind picks up, Peter panics and starts to sink. In Greek, the name Peter means "rock."

Peter, "the rock," sank when he looked to himself instead of to Jesus. Jesus later described Peter as a rock of the church (Matthew 16:18).

The Five Grossest
Bible Stories

1 Eglon and Ehud (Judges 3:12–30.)
Before kings reigned over Israel, judges ruled the people. At
that time, a very overweight king named Eglon conquered
Israel and demanded money. A man named Ehud brought
the payment to Eglon while he was perched on his "throne"
(meaning "toilet"). Along with the money, Ehud handed
over a little something extra — his sword, which he buried
so far in Eglon's belly that the sword disappeared into the
king's fat and, as the Bible says, "the dirt came out" (v. 22).

2 Job's sores (Job 2:1–10).
Job lived a righteous life yet he suffered anyway. He had
oozing sores from the bald spot on top of his head clear
down to the soft spot on the bottom of his foot. Job used a
broken piece of pottery to scrape away the pus that leaked
from his sores.

3 The naked prophet (Isaiah 20).
God's prophets went to great lengths to get God's message
across to the people. Isaiah was no exception. God's people
planned a war, but God gave it the thumbs down. Isaiah
marched around Jerusalem naked for three years as a sign
of what would happen if the people went to war.

Jeremiah strapped on some filthy underwear to show God could no longer be proud of the people.

Filthy underware

❹ The almost-naked prophet (Jeremiah 13:1–11).
God sent Jeremiah to announce that God could no longer be proud of the people. To make the point, Jeremiah bought a new pair of underclothes, wore them every day without washing them, and then buried them in the wet river sand. Later, he dug them up, strapped them on, and shouted that this is what has happened to the people who were God's pride!

❺ Spilling your guts (Matthew 27:1–8; Acts 1:16–19).
Judas betrayed Jesus and sold him out for thirty pieces of silver. He bought a field with the ill-gotten loot. Guilt-stricken, Judas walked out to the field, his belly swelled up until it burst, and his intestines spilled out on the ground.

Five Facts about Life in Old Testament Times

1 **Almost everyone wore sandals.**
They were called "sandals" because people walked on sand much of the time.

2 **There were no newspapers.**
People got news by hearing it from other people. Spreading important news was like a giant game of "telephone."

3 **It was dark.**
Homes, often tents, were typically lit at night by an oil lamp, if at all.

4 **You had to fetch your water, which was scarce.**
Rich folks had servants to carry it for them, but most people had to carry household water in jugs or leather bags, usually some distance, from a river or well.

5 **Life expectancy was short.**
Despite some long-lived exceptions described in the book of Genesis, such as Abraham (175 years) and Methuselah (969 years), few people lived past 50.

Sandals were made for walking on sand.

Ten Important Things
That Happened between
the Old and New Testaments

The period of time described in the Old Testament ended about four hundred years before Jesus' birth. The people of God kept living, believing, struggling, and writing during that period. Here are some of the important events that took place between the Testaments.

1 The Hebrew nation dissolved.
In 587 B.C., the Babylonians destroyed Jerusalem and Solomon's temple, and took the people into exile. Judah was never again an independent kingdom.

2 The people scattered.
After the exile to Babylon ended, the people of Judah moved to many different places. Some of them later came back, but many never did. Some of them lived in Babylon, some lived in Egypt, and some just scattered elsewhere.

3 A religion replaced a nation.
As a result of items 1 and 2, the people's religion changed. They no longer had a state or national religion (Judean religion). Instead, they had a freestanding faith called Judaism.

4 The Aramaic language became popular.
Because Aramaic was the international language of the Persian Empire, many Jews quit speaking Hebrew and spoke Aramaic instead. This is why Jesus spoke Aramaic.

❺ Alexander the Great conquered the world.
Around 330 B.C., Alexander the Great conquered the Mediterranean and Mesopotamian world. As a result, Greek became the everyday language of business and trade in the region. This is why the New Testament was written in Greek.

❻ The hammer dropped.
Around 170 B.C., the Seleucid emperor outlawed circumcision and the Sabbath and defiled the temple. A family of Jews called the Maccabees (which means "hammer") led a revolt.

❼ The Hebrew Scriptures were finished.
During this time, the individual books that make up what we call the Old Testament were finished. Several other religious books written at this time (mostly in Greek) aren't in the Protestant Bible but are part of the Apocrypha.

❽ The Sadducees, Pharisees, Essenes, Samaritans, Zealots, and other groups of people sprouted up.
Different schools of thought developed within Judaism. Most of their disagreements were over the idea that God's people would be resurrected to eternal life.

❾ God seemed to have forgotten the promise.
God promised King David that one of his descendants would always be king in Jerusalem. But after the Babylonian exile, there were no kings in Jerusalem. People wondered what had happened to God's promise.

❿ The Roman Empire expanded.
In 63 B.C., the Roman Empire conquered Palestine, having already conquered pretty much everyone else in the region. This is why the Roman Empire ruled the area during the time of Jesus and the New Testament.

Five Facts about Life in New Testament Times

❶ Synagogues were not always buildings.
For worship, Jesus' people gathered in all kinds of places, often outdoors. "Church" was any gathering of people for worship.

❷ Houses were boxy.
Most houses had a flat roof with an outside staircase leading to it. Inhabitants would sleep on the roof during hot weather.

Houses in New Testament times were boxy.

❸ Every town had a marketplace.
Usually there was just one marketplace per town, but one could buy almost everything needed to live.

❹ People ate a lot of fish.
The most common fish in the Sea of Galilee were catfish and carp. Roasting over a charcoal fire was the most common method of cooking.

❺ Dogs were shunned.
The Jewish people in Jesus' day did not keep dogs as pets. Dogs were considered unclean because they ate garbage and animal carcasses.

The Five Biggest Misconceptions about the Bible

❶ The Bible was written in a short period of time.
Christians believe that God inspired the Bible writers, the first of whom may have been Moses. God inspired people to write down important histories, traditions, songs, wise sayings, poetry, and prophetic words. All told — from the first recordings of the stories in Genesis to the last decisions about Revelation — the entire Bible formed over a period spanning anywhere from eight hundred to fourteen hundred years!

❷ One person wrote the Bible.
Unlike Islam's Koran, which was written by the prophet Muhammad, the books of the Bible claim the handiwork of many people. Much of Scripture does not identify the human hand that wrote it, so some parts of the Bible may have been written by women as well as men.

❸ The entire Bible should be taken literally.
While many parts of the Bible are meant as descriptions of actual historical events, other parts are intended as *illustrations of God's truth*, such as Song of Solomon, the book of Revelation, and Jesus' parable of the good Samaritan. So when Jesus says, "If your right eye causes you to sin, tear it out and throw it away" (Matthew 5:29), please do not take the saying literally!

❹ People in Bible times were unenlightened.

During the fourteen hundred years it took to write the Bible, some of history's greatest thinkers lived and worked. Many of these philosophers, architects, mathematicians, orators, theologians, historians, doctors, military tacticians, inventors, engineers, poets, and playwrights are still quoted today and their works are still in use.

❺ The Bible is a single book.

The Bible is actually a collection of books, letters, and other writings — more like a library than a book. There are thirty-nine books in the Hebrew Scriptures, what Christians call the "Old" Testament, and twenty-seven books (mostly letters) in the New Testament. There are seven books in the Apocryhpha (books written between the Old and New Testaments), or "deuterocanonical" books.

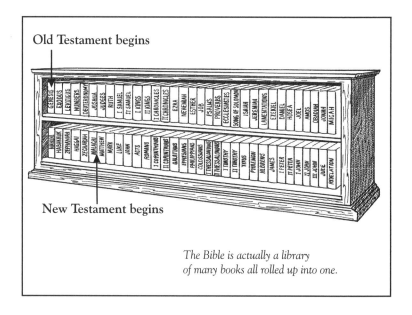

The Bible is actually a library of many books all rolled up into one.

Jesus' Twelve Apostles (plus Judas and Paul)

While Jesus had many disciples (students and followers) the Bible focuses particularly on twelve who were closest to him. Tradition says that these twelve spread Jesus' message throughout the known world (Matthew 28:18–20). For this reason, they were known as apostles, a word that means "sent ones."

❶ Andrew

A fisherman and the first disciple to follow Jesus, Andrew brought his brother, Simon Peter, to Jesus.

❷ Bartholomew

Also called Nathanael, tradition has it that he was martyred by being skinned alive.

❸ James the Elder

James, with John and Peter, was one of Jesus' closest disciples. Herod Agrippa killed James because of his faith, which made him a martyr (Acts 12:2).

❹ John

John (or one of his followers) is thought to be the author of the Gospel of John and three letters of John. He probably died of natural causes in old age.

❺ Matthew

Matthew was a tax collector and, therefore, probably an outcast even among his own people. He is attributed with the authorship of the Gospel of Matthew.

6 Peter

Peter was a fisherman who was brought to faith by his brother Andrew. He was probably martyred in Rome by being crucified upside down.

7 Philip

Philip, possibly a Greek, is responsible for bringing Bartholomew (Nathanael) to faith. He is thought to have died in a place called Phrygia.

8 James the Less

James was called "the Less" so he wouldn't be confused with James, the brother of John, or James, Jesus' brother.

9 Simon

Simon is often called "the Zealot." Zealots were a political group in Jesus' day that favored the overthrow of the Roman government by force.

10 Jude

Jude may have worked with Simon the Zealot in Persia (Iran) where they were martyred on the same day.

11 Thomas

"Doubting" Thomas preached the message of Jesus in India.

12 Matthias

Matthias was chosen by lot to replace Judas. It is thought that he worked mostly in Ethiopia.

⓭ Judas Iscariot

Judas was the treasurer for Jesus' disciples and the one who betrayed Jesus for thirty pieces of silver. According to the Bible, Judas killed himself for his betrayal.

⓮ Paul

Paul is considered primarily responsible for bringing non-Jewish people to faith in Jesus. He traveled extensively and wrote many letters to believers. Many of Paul's letters are included in the New Testament.

The Five Weirdest Laws in the Old Testament

The Old Testament has many helpful, commonsense laws, such as "You shall not kill," and "You shall not steal." But there are a few others that need some explaining.

❶ The "ox" law.
"When an ox gores a man or a woman to death, the ox shall be stoned, and its flesh shall not be eaten; but the owner of the ox shall not be liable" (Exodus 21:28). Replace "ox" with "car" and the law makes more sense — it is about protecting others from reckless actions.

People living in biblical times were sometimes gored by oxen.

People who were gored by oxen — or victims of other crimes — had legal recourse.

2 **The "no kid boiling" law.**

"You shall not boil a kid in its mother's milk" (Exodus 23:19b). A "kid," of course, is a juvenile goat, not a human being.

3 **The "which bugs are legal to eat" law.**

"All winged insects that walk upon all fours are detestable to you. But among the winged insects that walk on all fours you may eat those that have jointed legs above their feet" (Leviticus 11:20–21). The law is unclear whether it is legal to eat the bug if you first pull off the legs.

4 **The "don't eat blood" law.**

"No person among you shall eat blood" (Leviticus 17:12). Some laws beg the question whether people in that time had any sense of taste.

5 **The "pure cloth" law.**

"You shall not wear clothes made of wool and linen woven together" (Deuteronomy 22:11). Polyester came along after Bible times.

The Top Ten Bible Miracles and What They Mean

❶ Creation.
God created the universe and everything in it, and God continues to create and re-create without ceasing. God's first and ongoing miracle was to reveal that the creation has a purpose.

❷ The Passover.
The Israelites were enslaved by Pharaoh, a ruler who believed the people belonged to him, not to God. In the last of ten plagues, God visited the houses of all the Egyptians to kill the firstborn male in each one. God alone is Lord of the people, and no human can claim ultimate power over us.

❸ The Exodus.
God's people were fleeing Egypt when Pharaoh dispatched his army to force them back into slavery. The army trapped the people with their backs to a sea, but God parted the water and the people walked across to freedom while Pharaoh's minions were destroyed. God chose to free us from all forms of tyranny so we may use that freedom to serve God and each other.

❹ Manna.
After the people crossed the sea to freedom, they complained that they were going to starve to death. They even asked to go back to Egypt. God sent manna, a form of bread, so the people lived. God cares for us even when we give up, pine for our slavery, and lose faith. God never abandons us.

5 **The Incarnation.**

The immortal and infinite God became a human being, choosing to be born of a woman. God loved us enough to become one of us in Jesus of Nazareth, forever bridging the divide that had separated us from God.

6 **Jesus healed the paralyzed man.**

Some men brought a paralyzed friend to Jesus. Jesus said, "Son, your sins are forgiven" (Mark 2:5). This means that Jesus has the power to forgive our sins — and he does so as a free gift.

7 **Jesus calmed the storm.**

Jesus was asleep in a boat with his disciples when a great storm came up and threatened to sink it. He said, "Peace! Be still!" (Mark 4:39). Then the storm immediately calmed. Jesus is Lord over even the powers of nature.

8 **The Resurrection.**

Human beings executed Jesus, but God raised him from the dead on the third day. Through baptism, we share in Jesus' death, so we will also share in eternal life with God the Father, Son, and Holy Spirit. Christ conquered death.

9 **Pentecost.**

Jesus ascended from the earth, but he did not leave the church powerless or alone. On the fiftieth day after the Jewish Passover (Pentecost means fiftieth), Jesus sent the Holy Spirit to create the church and take up residence among us. The Holy Spirit is present with us always.

10 **The Second Coming.**

One day, Christ will come again and end all suffering. This means that the final result of the epic battle between good and evil is already assured. It is simply that evil has not yet admitted defeat.

The Exodus

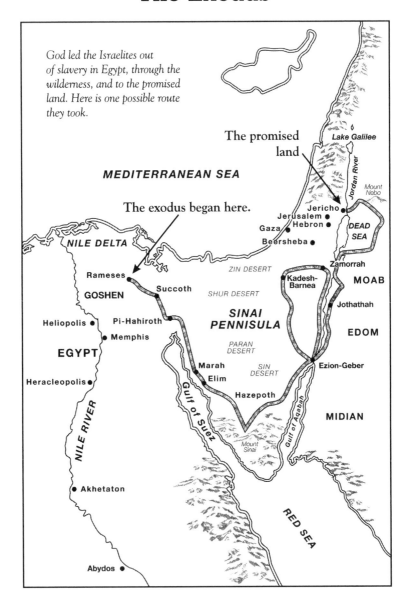

God led the Israelites out of slavery in Egypt, through the wilderness, and to the promised land. Here is one possible route they took.

The promised land

Lake Galilee

MEDITERRANEAN SEA

The exodus began here.

Jordan River

Mount Nebo

Jericho
Jerusalem ●
Gaza ● Hebron ●
Beersheba ●

DEAD SEA

NILE DELTA

ZIN DESERT

Zamorrah

Rameses
Succoth

SHUR DESERT

Kadesh-Barnea

MOAB

GOSHEN

SINAI PENNISULA

Jothathah

Heliopolis ●
Pi-Hahiroth
● Memphis

PARAN DESERT

EDOM

EGYPT

Marah
Elim

SIN DESERT

Ezion-Geber

Heracleopolis ●

Hazepoth

Gulf of Suez

Gulf of Aqabah

MIDIAN

NILE RIVER

Mount Sinai

● Akhetaton

RED SEA

● Abydos

The Holy Land:
Old Testament Times

The Holy Land:
New Testament Times

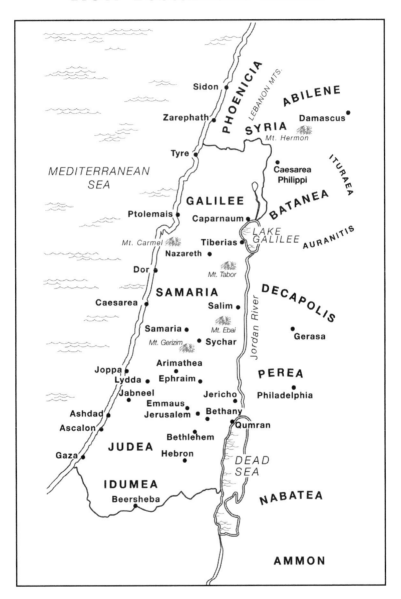

Jerusalem in Jesus' Time

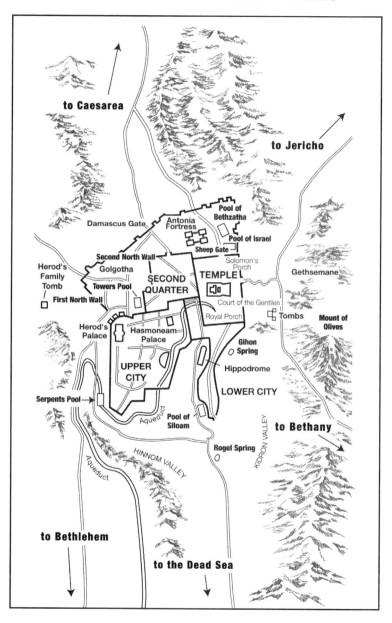

to Caesarea

to Jericho

Pool of Bethzatha

Antonia Fortress

Damascus Gate

Pool of Israel

Sheep Gate

Second North Wall

Solomon's Porch

Herod's Family Tomb

Golgotha

SECOND QUARTER

TEMPLE

Gethsemane

Towers Pool

First North Wall

Court of the Gentiles

Royal Porch

Tombs

Mount of Olives

Herod's Palace

Hasmoneam Palace

Gihon Spring

UPPER CITY

Hippodrome

LOWER CITY

Serpents Pool

Aqueduct

Pool of Siloam

KIDRON VALLEY

to Bethany

HINNOM VALLEY

Rogel Spring

Aqueduct

to Bethlehem

to the Dead Sea

Paul's Journeys

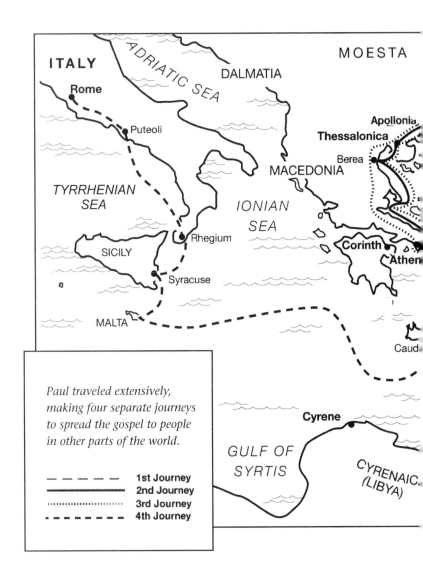

Paul traveled extensively, making four separate journeys to spread the gospel to people in other parts of the world.

— — — — — 1st Journey
——————— 2nd Journey
···················· 3rd Journey
- - - - - - - 4th Journey

THRACE

BLACK SEA

Philippi

Neapolis

Byzantium

Troas

ASIA

GALATIA

CAPPADOCIA

LYDIA

Sardis

Pisidian Antioch

Iconium

CHIOS

Ephesus

Colossae

Lystra

Derbe

Tarsus

Miletus

SAMOS

Cnidus

Attalia

Perga

Cos

Myra

Patara

Seleucia

CRETE

Salamis

Casea

CYPRUS

MEDITERRANEAN SEA

Sidon

Tyre

Ptolemais

Caesarea

Alexandria

Jerusalem

DEAD SEA

EGYPT

0   300 mi.

0   400 km.

Noah's Ark

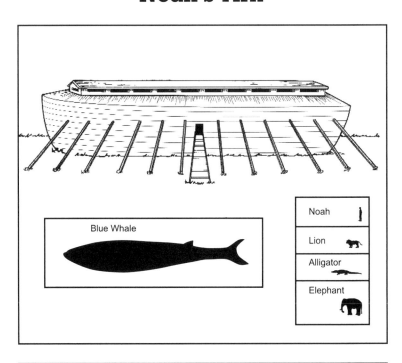

Blue Whale

Noah	
Lion	
Alligator	
Elephant	

A cubit is equal to the length of a man's forearm from the elbow to the tip of the middle finger — approximately 18 inches or 45.7 centimeters. Noah's ark was 300 cubits long, 50 cubits wide, and 30 cubits tall (Genesis 6:15).

One Cubit

The Ark of the Covenant

God told the Israelites to place the stone tablets—the "covenant"—
of the law into the Ark of the Covenant. The Israelites believed that
God was invisibly enthroned above the vessel and went before them
wherever they traveled.

The Ark of the Covenant was
2.5 cubits long and 1.5 cubits
wide (Exodus 25:17).

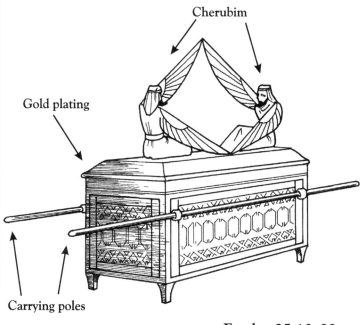

Cherubim

Gold plating

Carrying poles

Exodus 25:10–22

Solomon's Temple

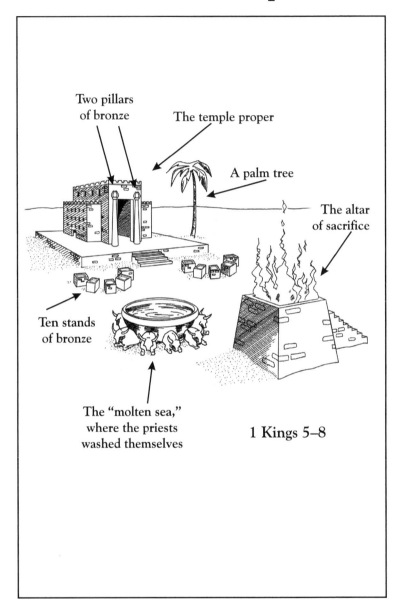

Two pillars of bronze

The temple proper

A palm tree

The altar of sacrifice

Ten stands of bronze

The "molten sea," where the priests washed themselves

1 Kings 5–8

The Armor of God

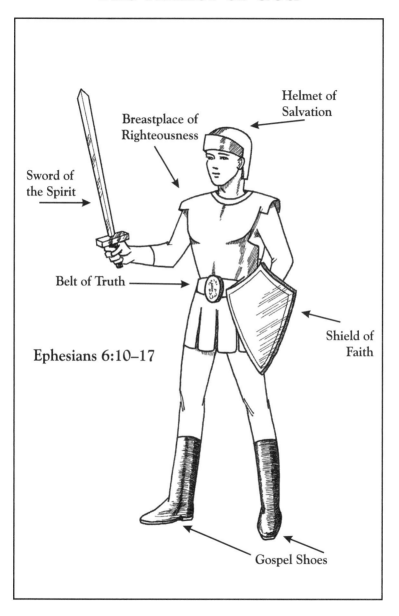

Helmet of Salvation

Breastplace of Righteousness

Sword of the Spirit

Belt of Truth

Ephesians 6:10–17

Shield of Faith

Gospel Shoes

The Passion and Crucifixion

Judas betrayed Jesus with a kiss, saying, "The one I will kiss is the man; arrest him" (Matthew 26:48).

Peter denied Jesus three times (Matthew 26:69–75).

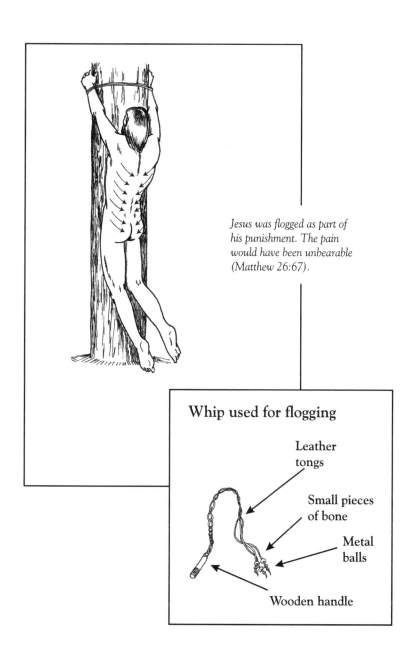

Jesus was flogged as part of his punishment. The pain would have been unbearable (Matthew 26:67).

Whip used for flogging

Leather tongs

Small pieces of bone

Metal balls

Wooden handle

After being flogged, carrying the patibulum was nearly impossible for Jesus.

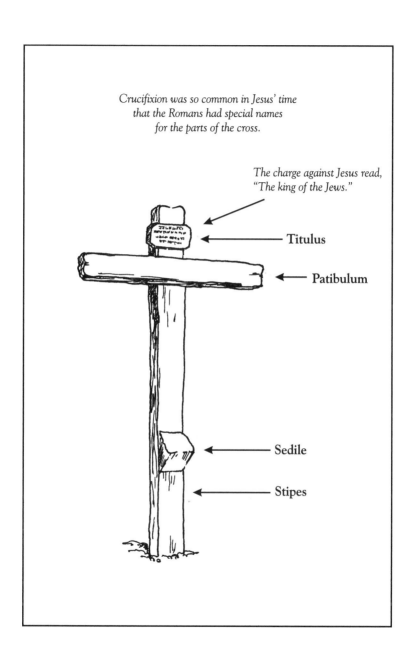

Crucifixion was so common in Jesus' time that the Romans had special names for the parts of the cross.

The charge against Jesus read, "The king of the Jews."

Titulus

Patibulum

Sedile

Stipes

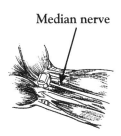

Median nerve

Typical crucifixion involved being nailed to the cross through the wrists— an excruciatingly painful and humiliating punishment.

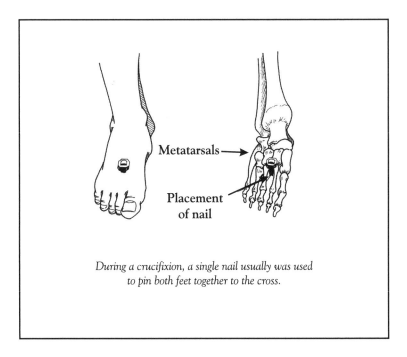

Metatarsals

Placement of nail

During a crucifixion, a single nail usually was used to pin both feet together to the cross.

Eventually, the victim would be unable to lift himself to take a breath, and he would suffocate.

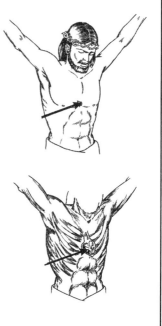

While the Romans broke the legs of the men who were crucified next to Jesus, they found that Jesus had already died. To make sure, they pierced his side with a spear, probably to puncture his heart (John 19:34).

UCC Stuff

The United Church of Christ likes to do things its own way, from the way we're organized to what we call stuff. Herewith, a brief compendium of boasts, confessions, explanations, guides, and history designed to help you navigate the heady, exasperating mix that is the UCC.

Ten Firsts of the United Church of Christ

❶ 1700: First Anti-Slavery Pamphlet
Judge Samuel Sewall of Boston writes the first anti-slavery pamphlet in America — partly in atonement for having sentenced several so-called "witches" to death in the Salem trials. Sewall lays the foundation for the abolitionist movement, which comes more than a century later and gives the rest of us hope that we can overcome our own sins with brave new acts.

❷ 1773: First act of civil disobedience
Five thousand angry colonists gather in Boston's Old South Meeting House to demand repeal of an unjust tax on tea. Their protest leads to the first act of civil disobedience in U.S. history — the "Boston Tea Party."

❸ 1773: First published African-American woman
A member of Old South Church in Boston, Phillis Wheatley becomes the first published African-American woman. "Poems on Various Subjects" is a sensation, and Wheatley gains her freedom from slavery soon after. Modern African-American poet Alice Walker says of her: "[She] kept alive, in so many of our ancestors, the notion of song."

❹ 1785: First ordained African-American pastor
Lemuel Haynes is the first African-American ordained by a Protestant denomination. He becomes a world-renowned preacher and writer.

---

❺ 1840: First united church in U.S. history
A meeting of Missouri pastors forms the first united church in U.S. history — the Evangelical Synod. It unites two Protestant traditions that have been separated for centuries: Lutheran and Reformed.

❻ 1846: First integrated anti-slavery society
The *Amistad* case is a spur to the conscience of Congregationalists who believe no human being should be a slave. In 1846 Lewis Tappan, one of the *Amistad* organizers, organizes the American Missionary Association — the first anti-slavery society in the U.S. with multiracial leadership.

❼ 1853: First woman pastor
Antoinette Brown is the first woman since New Testament times ordained as a Christian minister, and perhaps the first woman in history elected to serve a Christian congregation as pastor. At her ordination a friend, Methodist minister Luther Lee, defends "a woman's right to preach the gospel." He quotes the New Testament: "There is neither male nor female, for you are all one in Christ Jesus."

❽ 1972: First openly gay minister ordained
The UCC's Golden Gate Association ordains the first openly gay person as a minister in a mainline Protestant denomination: the Rev. William R. Johnson. In the following three decades, General Synod urges equal rights for homosexual citizens and calls on congregations to welcome gay, lesbian, and bisexual members.

⑨ 1976: First African-American leader of an integrated denomination
General Synod elects the Rev. Joseph H. Evans president of the United Church of Christ. He becomes the first African-American leader of a racially integrated mainline church in the United States.

⑩ 1995: First gender inclusive hymnal
The UCC publishes *The New Century Hymnal* — the first and only hymnal released by a Christian church that honors in equal measure both male and female images of God. Although its poetry is contemporary, its theology is traditional.

Our Bad:
A Couple of Moments in United Church of Christ History We Would Change If We Owned a Delorean and a Flux Capacitor

Salem witch trials of 1692

For almost a year, fear and accusation ruled some Congregationalist communities. "I saw (insert name of your nemesis here) consorting with the Devil!"

- In 1692 the daughter and niece of Congregationalist minister Reverend Samuel Parris became ill and were diagnosed (by a doctor no less) with "bewitchment."

- From March 1, 1692, until the trials ended in January 1693, 19 people were hanged, 1 pressed to death, and as many as 13 died in prison. Overall, 140 people were accused of witchcraft.

- To the good, however, the trials came to an end when respected ministers started to believe that some innocent people were being accused and executed for witchcraft. They joined together and put an end to the practice using "spectral evidence." As the Reverend Increase Mather stated, "It were better than ten suspected witches should escape than one innocent person should be condemned."

- You're welcome, Arthur Miller and Joseph McCarthy, for making "witch hunting" highly profitable.

No actual Wiccans were harmed in the making of this moment in history.

The overthrow of Queen Lili'uokalani in 1893

• Starting in 1820 Christian missionaries began arriving in Hawaii, sent there by the American Board of Commissioners for Foreign Missions of the Congregational Churches (a predecessor denomination of the UCC).

• In 1893 Queen Lili'uokalani, was overthrown by American citizens backed by U.S. Marines. Although the missionaries themselves were not around at the time of the overthrow, children of the missionaries, the Christian church tradition, and the churches themselves had a role to play in what took place in 1893.

• In January 17, 1993, then president of the UCC, Paul Sherry, made a public apology on behalf of the entire UCC to the native Hawaiian people, thus beginning a process of reconciliation. The UCC also pledged and delivered financial redress. The U.S. government would later issue a similar apology — but no financial redress.

UCC Jargon: The 411 on UCC Acronyms and Ideas

I Know I Am, But What Are You? Church Designations

ONA: After going through a process of study and discernment, a congregation may feel called to adopt a statement proclaiming itself **Open** (to) **& Affirming** (of) [ONA] people who are gay, lesbian, bisexual, transgender, and maybe more.

Just Peace: Ditto, but here the proclamation is that the congregation is committed to building peace based on justice and not on coercion or misuse of power.

Multiracial/Multicultural: Ditto, but for intentionally striving to be made up of many races and cultures not just in the pews, but in worship style, song choices, and more.

Accessible to All: Ditto, but probably costs more money than the others. This one is all about making people of different ability levels feel at home and may involve putting in ramps and elevators, buying large-print hymnals, hiring American Sign Language interpreters, and more.

Your Favorite: There are lots more of these out there, and we've probably offended you by leaving yours out. Un-offend yourself by writing it in here:

_____

_____

The "Big Five" National Offerings

Our Church's Wider Mission (OCWM) is the primary way that other parts of the church receive money from local churches and individuals. From Global Ministries to National Offices to conferences, OCWM makes everything UCC outside of your local church — cool pamphlets, bumper stickers, websites, advertising, conference events, camps, resources, and more — possible.

Four Special Offerings

Neighbors in Need (NIN) supports ministries of justice and compassion in the United States. Do you like seeing leading UCC folks getting arrested for a good cause? It's probably NIN money that got them there just in time to be zip-cuffed in front of the cameras.

Christmas Fund (formerly Veterans of the Cross): At one time most ministers didn't make much cash. It's tough to retire on a steady stream of homemade goodies, homegrown produce, and thank you notes. The Christmas Fund helps out retirees as well as current ministers and employees in need.

One Great Hour of Sharing (OGHS): The UCC buddies up with many other denominations to take this special offering all on the same Sunday to support ministries of justice and compassion in more than eighty countries.

Strengthen the Church does just what it says by funneling funds back to local churches to support them, their leaders, and their members.

Other Jargon about the Wider Church

Settings: Sometimes in a church with congregational polity, we can get to believing that the only real church is the local one. Against such a notion, we say that the church has many settings: local church, association (small group of churches), conference (grouping of churches and associations), and national, all of which are fully and equally church, they just can't tell each other what to do or believe. Not an elegant term, but it works.

Collegium: The national setting is made up of several sections, each of which has an executive. These executives (there are four at this writing, but you never know when a reorganization is going to happen around here!) gather in an executive body called the Collegium of Officers. First among these equals is the general minister and president, our chief executive (but not the Head of the Church; that's Jesus).

General Synod: A synod is a gathering of church representatives. Every two years, representatives from all across the UCC gather for this denomination-wide meeting, at which we elect officers, make pronouncements on issues of the day, and do other institutional business — as well as give Hawaiians and Vermonters a chance to worship and party together.

Soft Verbs: We say we're a denomination of soft verbs because in our organization, no one setting can make or force (those are hard verbs) any other setting to do anything. General Synod can exhort, encourage, invite, beg your local church to do something or believe something. But unless your church is convinced Jesus wants them to do it, they don't have to.

Show Me the Money:
The Flow of Funds through
the United Church of Christ

In any organization, if you want to know where the power is, follow the money. We may wish it wasn't true, but even in churches, whoever controls the money has the power. The diagram on the following page proves once and for all just who calls the shots around here.

Notice that all the money comes from the local churches and filters "down" to higher levels of organization, leaving the denominational executives to hope for the best when it comes to their budgeting — and to listen carefully to what the local churches have to say. A far cry from *some* ecclesiastical structures we could name!

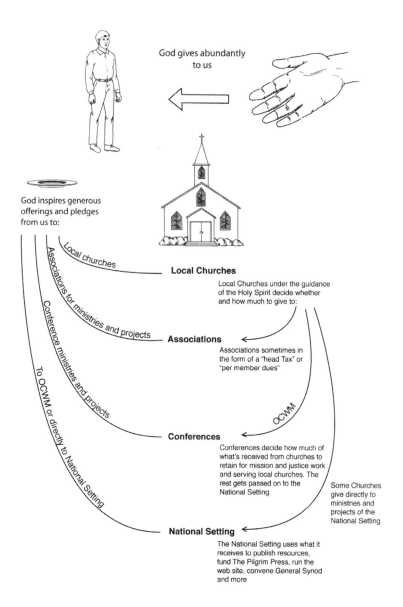

God gives abundantly
to us

God inspires generous
offerings and pledges
from us to:

Local churches

Associations for ministries and projects

Conference ministries and projects

To OCWM or directly to National Setting

Local Churches

Local Churches under the guidance
of the Holy Spirit decide whether
and how much to give to:

Associations

Associations sometimes in
the form of a "head Tax" or
"per member dues"

OCWM

Conferences

Conferences decide how much of
what's received from churches to
retain for mission and justice work
and serving local churches. The
rest gets passed on to the
National Setting

Some Churches
give directly to
ministries and
projects of the
National Setting

National Setting

The National Setting uses what it
receives to publish resources,
fund The Pilgrim Press, run the
web site, convene General Synod
and more

Are You There, God?
It's Me, Church

Democracy

Each person votes
his or her conscience

Each person has a
vote because of a
notion of intrinsic
worth

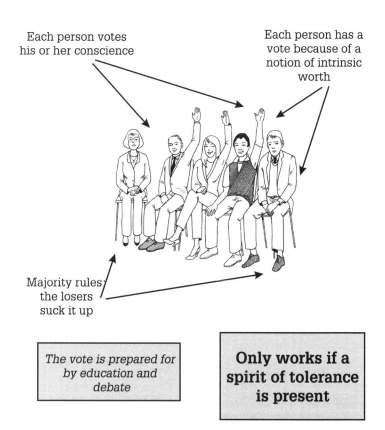

Majority rules
the losers
suck it up

*The vote is prepared for
by education and
debate*

**Only works if a
spirit of tolerance
is present**

In a congregational polity like ours, each part of the church (local congregations, associations, conferences, the national setting, and more) makes its own decisions about matters both important and un-. This work is done in meetings where the members or other constituents vote. If you just glance at it, this can look like democracy. Look closer, and you'll see it's something else.

Congregational Way

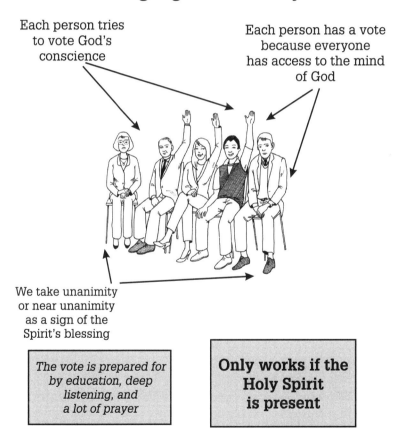

Each person tries to vote God's conscience

Each person has a vote because everyone has access to the mind of God

We take unanimity or near unanimity as a sign of the Spirit's blessing

The vote is prepared for by education, deep listening, and a lot of prayer

Only works if the Holy Spirit is present

Whitewater Rafting down the Four Streams: A Ridiculously Concise and Oversimplified History of the United Church of Christ

The history of the UCC is as long and complex as that of the United States itself. In many ways, we are the first truly American denomination. That said, one way to talk about our history is to look at four great streams that came together when the UCC was formed in 1957. There are lots of other streams and "hidden histories" that have come together as well, but we'll stick to just the four.

Evangelical

* **In a nutshell:** Germans arriving on the American frontier in the nineteenth century brought with them pietism (religion of the heart), a mix of Lutheran and Reformed faith, missionary zeal, and a yearning for peace in reaction to the religious wars in Germany. Eventually coalesced into the Evangelical Synod of North America, it merged with the Reformed Church in the United States in 1934.

* **Center of gravity:** Midwest.

* **What you might expect if you visit one:** Strong sense of ethnic German heritage, perhaps including an annual service in German. Traditional Church buildings that recall German architecture and decoration, with dark carved wood and stained glass. Balance of Lutheran and Reformed thinking with an emphasis on individual conscience and liberty.

- **What they bring to the party:** Indefinable, but tasty casseroles.

- **Closest living non-UCC relatives:** Lutherans.

Reformed

- **In a nutshell:** Germans arriving in Pennsylvania at the turn of the century brought the Heidelberg Catechism, pragmatic concerns, and no pastors. For years they managed just fine with lay leaders, thank you, until regularly ordained pastors began to arrive from the old world. Merged with the Evangelical Synod of North America in 1934.

- **Center of gravity:** Pennsylvania and the mid-Atlantic.

- **What you might expect if you visit one:** Ditto to the Evangelicals. Commitment to the best of the traditional Reformed faith, perhaps including the Heidelberg Catechism, formal litanies, chants, prayers, and an emphasis on sacraments.

- **What they bring to the party:** A playlist of familiar but utterly undanceable tunes.

- **Closest living non-UCC relatives:** Reformed Church in America.

Congregational

- **In a nutshell:** English Puritans and Pilgrims founded autonomous congregations marked by strict Calvinist belief, plain worship stripped of all smells and bells, the Protestant ethic, and a commitment to learning. Many merged with the Christian churches in 1931.

- **Center of gravity:** New England.

- **What you might expect if you visit one:** Virtually uniformly Anglo-Saxon old guard with a diverse younger mix, all with a strong "you're not the boss of me" streak. Plain white church buildings (or "meeting houses") with little interior decoration, clear glass windows, and a high, central pulpit. Worship with a focus on preaching.

- **What they bring to the party:** A list of relatives who were on the *Mayflower*.

- **Closest living non-UCC relatives:** Unitarian Universalists; Continuing Congregational Churches.

Christian

- **In a nutshell:** Riding high on the heart-centered Second Great Awakening, several different groups tired of the burdens and strictures placed on them by affiliation with existing denominations and broke away. They called themselves simply "Christian" and sought to create a faithful way of being appropriate to their new frontier circumstances. "No creed but Christ, no book but the Bible" was one rallying cry. Merged with many Congregational churches in 1931.

- **Center of gravity:** Virginia and Kentucky (at that time, the frontier), with significant outposts in New England and Ohio.

- **What you might expect if you visit one:** Commitment to God and a love of Communion mark most of these congregations. Beyond that, don't bother expecting much; this is a diverse bunch!

- **What they bring to the party:** Wine, bread, and some guy they just met on the street.

- **Closest living non-UCC relatives:** The Christian Church (Disciples of Christ), with whom the UCC shares a global missions board.

Goliaths:
Four UCC Intellectual Giants Not to Sling a Stone at (But If You Think You've Got the Stuff, Bucky, Give It a Shot)

Cotton Mather (1663–1728)

As a scion of two great Boston Puritan families (the Cottons and the Mathers) with more ministers in them than you could shake a stick at, it was pretty much guaranteed that young Cotton would become a minister too. Not to mention that he was brilliant, widely read, and much-respected. He wrote over four hundred books, set the moral tone for the age, helped introduce smallpox inoculation to the Colonies, had a hand in the trials of the so-called Salem witches (which, depending on whom you ask, he either helped tone down or made way worse), all while pastoring Boston's Second Church, marrying three wives, and fathering fifteen children.

- ◆ **Quotable Mather:** "Ah! destructive Ignorance, what shall be done to chase thee out of the World!"

Jonathan Edwards (1703–1758)

Another scion of a ministerial family, Edwards came from Connecticut to take over his grandfather's Congregational church in Northampton, Massachusetts. There, he would initiate the First Great Awakening and grow to become one of the greatest American philosophers and theologians of all time. His uncharacteristically fire-and-brimstone-y sermon "Sinners in the Hands of an Angry God" is a classic of early American literature.

- **Quotable Edwards:** "Such little things as Christians commonly do will not evince much increase in grace. We must do great things for God."

Harriet Beecher Stowe (1811–1896)

Daughter of one minister, sister to some seven others (are you noticing a pattern here?), her novel *Uncle Tom's Cabin* changed the course of a nation. Few single books have so radically affected history. She wrote more than twenty other books, as well as touring and lecturing on causes from emancipation to temperance.

- **Quotable Stowe:** "One would like to be grand and heroic, if one could; but if not, why try at all? One wants to be very something, very great, very heroic; or if not that, then at least very stylish and very fashionable. It is this everlasting mediocrity that bores me."

Reinhold Niebuhr (1892–1972)

The son of a pastor (seriously, are you noticing anything?), he served a hardscrabble Detroit parish for many years before going on to become the nation's most famous theologian of the middle part of the twentieth century and one of its most important public intellectuals. He called on liberals to discard idealism in modern politics and on conservatives to move away from narrow social views. America listened when Niebuhr talked — and he talked (and wrote) a lot, when he wasn't doing things like posing for the cover of *Time* or authoring the world-famous Serenity Prayer.

- **Quotable Niebuhr:** "Man's capacity for justice makes democracy possible; but man's inclination to injustice makes democracy necessary."

United Not Uniform

A lot of people ask, "So what does the UCC believe?" The usual response is something like, "It depends." Heck, if Jesus chose a zealot, a tax collector, and a couple of fisherman among his most trusted band, who are we to say we all have to agree all the time? One thing we agree on is that a church should be a place where we disagree mightily and still like being together. Everyone thinking the same is just plain boring anyway. Some issues where you'll find a difference of opinion in the UCC include:

Stance	Issue	Stance
Pro-Choice	Abortion	Pro-Life
Same Sex Marriage	Marriage	Only a Man and a Woman
Comprehensive Sex Ed	Sex Education	Abstinence Only Sex Ed
"Preach it, sister!"	Women's Role in Church	"Silence, woman!"
Human record of relationship with God	Bible	God wrote it without errors
Care for creation	Ecology	"mmm, bald eagles taste great!"
"Why kill to teach killing is wrong?"	Death Penalty	"Eye for an eye, it's in the Bible"
"Sounds good on a pipe organ"	Music	"Sounds good on the radio, why not in church?"
Old School	Worship Style	Fancy and Fresh
"Y'all Come"	Communion	"Baptized and of a certain age"

We invite you to locate yourself on this continuum of belief

←——————————————————————————————→

Fun with Letters:
Alternative Meanings of "UCC"

Untied Church of Christ

◆ When did a disorganized organizational structure become a bad thing? Don't confuse unity with uniformity. Because we value both the autonomy of local bodies and the covenant between them, this can get messy. After all, it's about *who* we are, not *how* we are.

Unlimited Coffee and Cookies

◆ Most UCC churches offer some time before or after worship to get to know people better. The church *is* a lot about relationship building. What better way to forge a longstanding friendship than bad (but fairly traded) coffee, powdered creamer, and some old sandwich cookies?

Unitarians Considering Christ

◆ Sure, we have a few sneaky Unitarians in our midst, but most UCCers are committed to following Jesus and think he was something special, even divine. Why settle for one face of God when you can have three? The UCC is a big tent with a clear center but flexible edges. A diversity of opinions and beliefs is one of the great things about being UCC. Go ahead and celebrate it!

A Bunch of Smart Alecs:
United Church of Christ Schools

The Pilgrims wanted a well-educated clergy. Just sixteen years after arriving they founded Harvard College in 1636. It's named after a young minister, John Harvard, who was the college's first benefactor.

In 1701 a group of Congregationalist ministers founded what became Yale University because of the belief that Harvard had gotten too lax and liberal with Puritan theology.

While few would acknowledge it now, nearly all of the nation's oldest and most prestigious colleges and universities were founded by UCC predecessor denominations and ministers.

Additionally, at the end of the Civil War, through the American Missionary Association, the Congregational Church set up over five hundred schools and academies for the "freedmen" who were liberated by slavery but uneducated because of the racism in the country that made it a crime to teach an African how to read. Of the five hundred plus schools that were set up, there are eight that are still in existence today (see *www.ucc.org/50/pdfs/wright.pdf*).

Nineteen schools are currently affiliated with the United Church of Christ. Another nine are considered "historically affiliated."

Colleges and Universities

Catawba College
Salisbury, NC
www.catawba.edu

Defiance College
Defiance, OH
www.defiance.edu

Dillard University
New Orleans, LA
www.dillard.edu

Doane College
Crete, NE
www.doane.edu

Drury University
Springfield, MO
www.drury.edu

Elmhurst College
Elmhurst, IL
www.elmhurst.edu

Elon University
Elon, NC
www.elon.edu

Heidelberg College
Tiffin, OH
www.heidelberg.edu

Huston-Tillotson University
Austin, TX
www.htu.edu

Illinois College
Jacksonville, IL
www.ic.edu

Lakeland College
Sheboygan, WI
www.lakeland.edu

Lemoyne-Owen College
Memphis, TN
www.loc.edu

Northland College
Ashland, WI
www.northland.edu

Olivet College
Olivet, MI
www.olivetcollege.edu

Pacific University
Forest Grove, OR
www.pacificu.edu

Piedmont College
Demorest, GA
www.piedmont.edu

Rocky Mountain College
Billings, MT
www.rocky.edu

Talladega College
Talladega, AL
www.talladega.edu

Tougaloo College
Tougaloo, MS
www.tougaloo.edu

Historical Member Colleges

Beloit College
Beloit, WI
www.beloit.edu

Cedar Crest College
Allentown, PA
www.cedarcrest.edu

Carleton College
Northfield, MN
www.carleton.edu

Chamberlain College
of Nursing
St. Louis, MO
www.chamberlain.edu

Fisk University
Nashville, TN
www.fisk.edu

Grinnell College
Grinnell, IA
www.grinnell.edu

Hood College
Frederick, MD
www.hood.edu

Ripon College
Ripon, WI
www.ripon.edu

Westminster College
of Salt Lake City
Salt Lake City, UT
www.wcslc.edu

The Mayflower Compact

"For the General Good": An Old and Novel Idea

Even before the Pilgrims landed, they recognized they'd need some kind of agreement about how to live together. On November 11, 1620, before they set foot on land, they drew up and signed the Mayflower Compact. Though it was a document to create a civil government, remember that these guys weren't interested in the separation of church and state. The Compact was in effect an early statement that a local body gathered far from hierarchies and centers of control had the right to band together and govern itself under God's lordship — the very tenet on which all Congregationalism is based.

In the name of God, Amen. We, whose names are under-written, the Loyal Subjects of our dread Sovereign Lord, King James, by the Grace of God, of England, France and Ireland, King, Defender of the Faith, etc. Having undertaken for the Glory of God, and Advancement of the Christian Faith, and the Honour of our King and Country, a voyage to plant the first colony in the northern parts of Virginia; do by these presents, solemnly and mutually in the Presence of God and one of another, covenant and combine ourselves together into a civil Body Politick, for our better Ordering and Preservation, and Furtherance of the Ends aforesaid; And by Virtue hereof to enact, constitute, and frame, such just and equal Laws, Ordinances, Acts, Constitutions and Offices, from time to time, as shall be thought most meet and convenient for the General good of the Colony; unto which we promise all due submission and obedience. In Witness whereof we have hereunto subscribed our names at Cape Cod the eleventh of November, in the Reign of our Sovereign Lord, King James of England, France and Ireland, the eighteenth, and of Scotland the fifty-fourth. Anno Domini, 1620.

Ever since then, UCC folks have been trying to figure out how to follow Jesus in such a way that we "covenant and combine ourselves together" for the general good.

Preamble to the Constitution of the United Church of Christ

When the UCC was created in 1957, the people in charge of such things knew that we would need to state what things, exactly, held such a disparate group together. Their best attempt to articulate these things came in the second paragraph of the Preamble to our Constitution:

The United Church of Christ acknowledges as its sole head, Jesus Christ, Son of God and Savior. It acknowledges as kindred in Christ all who share in this confession. It looks to the Word of God in the Scriptures, and to the presence and power of the Holy Spirit, to prosper its creative and redemptive work in the world. It claims as its own the faith of the historic Church expressed in the ancient creeds and reclaimed in the basic insights of the Protestant Reformers. It affirms the responsibility of the Church in each generation to make this faith its own in reality of worship, in honesty of thought and expression, and in purity of heart before God. In accordance with the teaching of our Lord and the practice prevailing among evangelical Christians, it recognizes two sacraments: Baptism and the Lord's Supper or Holy Communion.